D0590423

TRADITIONAL SLOW COOKING

TRADITIONAL SLOW COOKING

Eve Parker

AURA

This edition published in 2012
by Baker & Taylor (UK) Limited,
Bicester, Oxfordshire

26/27 Bickels Yard, 151–153 Bermondsey Street
London SE1 3HA

ISBN: 978-1-90723-128-5
AD002228EN

Printed in China

CONTENTS

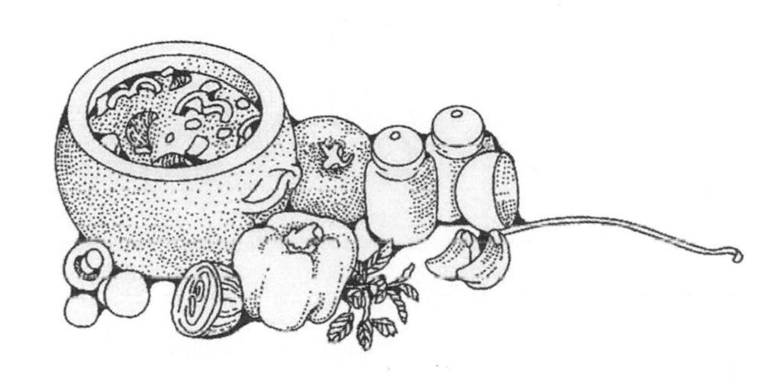

INTRODUCTION

These days, many people juggle looking after their home and children around a full-time job. For this very reason the slow cooker has enjoyed a revival in recent years, and has become a useful piece of equipment for fast-paced, modern-day life.

The joy of the slow cooker is the fact that when you come home after a busy day, there is a hot meal waiting for you. Just as our ancestors used to hang a cooking pot over a fire and leave it to bubble away all day, the slow cooker will do the job for you without you having to adjust the heat or worry about the food burning, and you know that at the end you will have a moist, succulent meal that is tender and full of flavour. Learning to balance the right flavours might take some experimenting, but once you have got the hang of using your slow cooker you will never look back.

The art of cooking food slowly in a single pot went into decline with the gradual introduction of controllable range cookers and eventually gas and electric ovens, which were designed to cook food faster. Then came the microwave and ready-prepared microwave meals that relieved busy mothers of hours of preparation, and what some considered to be the drudgery of cooking.

However, over time many people have become concerned about exactly what is going into these ready-prepared meals, particularly where children are concerned. Good home cooking has become popular once more and people have started to take greater care in what they are preparing and putting on the

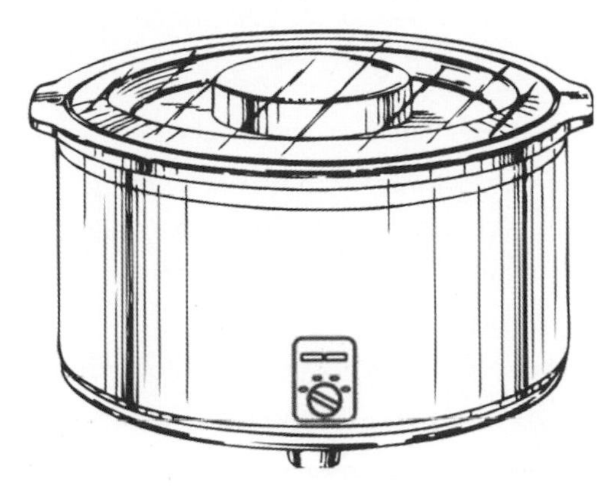

table. Yet with fewer full-time homemakers, ways of saving precious time have to be found and the slow cooker has come back into favour – so if you already have one sitting at the back of a cupboard gathering dust, now is the time to get it out.

WHAT IS A SLOW COOKER?

The slow cooker, also referred to as the slo-cooker or crock pot, is a round, or often oval, deep cooking pot that is made of strengthened, glazed ceramic or porcelain. The pot itself sits inside a metal unit that contains an electric element that can be set to cook on low, medium or high. The unit comes with a glass lid so that you can see the food cooking without having to lift it and let out the heat built up inside. Slow cookers come in varying sizes, so whatever the size of your family you should find one to suit you.

Because the slow cooker relies on extended cooking at low temperatures, you can use cheaper cuts of meat as they will tenderize as they cook slowly in their own juices. The addition of a liquid to the recipe, whether it is stock, water, wine, cider or beer, is important as it helps to carry the heat from the walls of the cooker to the food.

If you're concerned about leaving a piece of electrical equipment unattended while you're out at work, there's no need to be – the element uses less electricity than a standard light bulb, so it is economical and safe at the same time.

Many slow cookers come with built-in timers which can be switched to a setting to keep the food warm if your family don't all sit down to eat at the same time. This solves the problem of how to keep food hot and avoids you having to hurry home to turn off the slow cooker.

WHAT CAN BE COOKED IN A SLOW COOKER?

There is a misconception that only stews and casseroles can be cooked in a slow cooker. In fact, nothing could be further than the truth – its uses are surprisingly wide-ranging. Because of its gentle cooking action, the slow cooker won't spoil delicate foods such as fish, fruit or vegetables and they will remain intact even after several hours of cooking. Most recipes can be adapted for the slow cooker, including rice, pasta, soups, and even some delicious puddings. It can even be used as a *bain-marie*, or water bath, to produce creamy custards, sponge puddings or delicious pâtés.

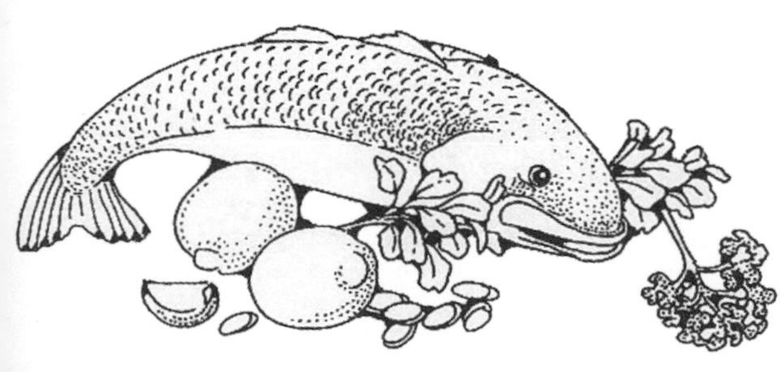

As each brand of slow cooker will be slightly different, it's important to get used to the settings on yours. If you are new to this style of cooking, start with the basic recipes and then progress to the more involved ones once you have gained confidence. None of the recipes included in this book is complicated – just follow the simple instructions and you will find a wide choice of meals to serve to your family. As your skill grows you will discover just how versatile slow cooking can be; it will let you learn to love the art of cooking and the simple joy of eating leisurely homemade meals with family and friends.

PART 1

GETTING STARTED

This extremely easy form of cooking has the added advantage of being environmentally friendly as it uses a much smaller amount of electricity than a conventional oven. It is, as its name suggests, a simple way of cooking food slowly, and it does it without any risk of burning the food.

LEARNING THE BASICS

This section gives you a guide as to how to use your slow cooker so that you make the most of its features and also offers advice on how to adapt your favourite recipes.

CHOOSING YOUR SLOW COOKER

The first priority is to choose a slow cooker that is the right size for your requirements. They come in a range of sizes from a small 600ml/1 pint to an enormous 6.5 litres/11¼ pints. For an average family of four, it is probably best to choose one of medium size, holding 3.5 litres/6 pints. As a guide, the manufacturers recommend that the pot should be filled at least halfway up for best results. Whichever size you choose, you can rest assured that it will take up very little space on your worktop, which means that you won't have to constantly put it away in a cupboard when you've finished using it.

If you are buying one of the smaller-capacity slow cookers, then shape is not really a priority. These are ideal for people who live on their own and don't intend to make large quantities. However, if you do need one with a larger capacity, then it's best to go for an oval shape as this means you can fit a whole chicken, a large joint of meat or an entire fish inside with ease and still have room for the vegetables.

Only buy a slow cooker that has a recognized safety mark for your particular country, as this means it has gone through stringent safety checks.

HOW DOES A SLOW COOKER WORK?

The outer casing of the slow cooker is metal and contains the heating element which, when heated up, transfers heat indirectly to warm the inner pot, or 'crock'. On most slow cookers there are LOW and HIGH settings; on LOW, the food is kept at a temperature of about 80–90°C/180–200°F and on HIGH the temperature is about 150°C/300°F. The latter is convenient if you want to speed up the cooking process. The constant, low temperature means the cooker can safely be left unsupervised for the times recommended in the recipes.

As the food cooks it releases steam and creates a vacuum seal between the rim of the crock and the lid, keeping the food moist even after hours of cooking. It is very hard to overcook food in a slow cooker, so even someone who has little experience of cooking can produce a delicious meal with very little effort.

CROCKS AND LIDS

The crock of the slow cooker is always removable, which makes it very easy to clean. There are no sharp corners for the food to get stuck in and some crocks are even designed to be put into the dishwasher. The majority are made from glazed ceramic because of its ability to retain heat. Some of the deluxe varieties come with a non-stick insert which can be used for browning meat or onions on the stove top or in the oven before putting them into the crock, which is not suitable for heating on the stove top.

Choose a crock that has sturdy handles to make your life easier when you are lifting it out with oven gloves.

A lid is a vital part of the slow cooker as it not only keeps the heat in but also allows condensation to drip back into the food, thereby stopping it from drying out. The lid is nearly always made of glass so that you can see how cooking is progressing without removing it. If you were to regularly lift the lid to check what stage the food was at you would need to increase the cooking time by at least 30–40 minutes to allow for the loss of heat.

Some slow cookers have a lid with a silicon seal and clips to hold it closed. This is by no means essential, but if you intend to move the pot around after cooking it can come in handy.

TEMPERATURE CONTROL AND PROGRAMMING

The majority of slow cookers have three settings – OFF, LOW and HIGH – but this will vary from model to model. Some of the more expensive ones will have a MEDIUM setting and also an AUTO, which automatically heats the cooker up to HIGH; when it reaches this point it will be maintained for some of the cooking period and then the temperature will be reduced to LOW to retain the heat for the remaining time.

It is also possible to buy some models with a programmable digital control which allows you to set the times you wish the cooker to come on and switch off. The maximum cooking time is usually 12 or 24 hours, in increments of 30 minutes or 1 hour, depending on the model you choose.

Some slow cookers switch automatically to WARM when the cooking time is complete. This is handy if you know you are going to be out all day, but not essential as the food will not spoil if left on LOW a little longer. Buying a slow cooker with this feature is a matter of choice.

All models have an indicator light that stays on during the cooking period, although some may go out after the desired temperature has been reached. Check the manufacturer's instructions if you are unsure.

A QUICK GUIDE TO THE SETTINGS

Low

This is the best setting to use if you are cooking cheaper cuts of red meat. You should allow between 8 and 12 hours on this setting; refer to the recommended time in the recipe.

Medium (Med)

Medium heat is used when you want to cook something a little faster without losing any of the benefits of slow cooking. Not all models have this option.

High (Hi)

This is usually recommended for cooking pale meats such as chicken or turkey. The recommended cooking times vary between 3 and 6 hours, or as recommended by the recipe.

Keep warm

An option only on certain models, this is designed to keep the finished meal from drying out if you know you are going to be late home.

Preheating programme

Some manufacturers recommend preheating the crock for 15–20 minutes before adding the ingredients. If you are unsure whether your model has this requirement, read the manufacturer's instructions carefully before using it for the first time. If your slow cooker does require you to do this, you will simply need to put the crock into the base then turn the setting up to HIGH for the required time while you prepare the ingredients.

CARE OF YOUR SLOW COOKER

The general rule is to take care of your slow cooker and it will take care of you.

- Before you use your crock and lid for the first time, give them a wash in hot, soapy water and then dry thoroughly.
- Never use abrasive cleaners or scouring pads to clean your slow cooker.
- Do not put the crock in the

dishwasher unless the manufacturer's instructions say this is safe.

- Remove any residue from the crock with a cloth, sponge or rubber spatula.
- Never subject your crock or lid to sudden changes in temperature. For example, do not plunge the crock into cold water when it is hot or pour boiling water into it when it is cold as this could lead to cracking.
- Always make sure you turn off your slow cooker after use. Unplug it from the wall and allow it to cool down before cleaning. The base may be cleaned with a soft cloth and warm, soapy water.
- Never immerse the heating base in water.
- Take care when handling the lid and crock after use as both will be exceptionally hot. Always use a pair of oven gloves if you are transferring the crock to the table.
- Don't be concerned if you notice fine cracks appearing in the glaze of the crock after a few months' usage; this is quite normal and will not affect the efficiency of your slow cooker. The only time the crock will need to be replaced is if it cracks enough that liquid can seep through.
- Make sure the electrical cord is long enough to reach the available socket without it being pulled taut.

WHY USE A SLOW COOKER?

There are many advantages to cooking with a slow cooker and once you have used it for a couple of months you will wonder how you lived without it.

- It will save you money on energy as it uses so little power, even on the highest setting.
- The slow cooker will not make your kitchen uncomfortably hot like a conventional oven can.
- It takes up very little space on your worktop.
- You can buy cheaper cuts of meat as the long, slow cooking

breaks down the collagen in the connective tissue, resulting in tender meat.

- There is very little washing up as everything is prepared and put straight into the crock.
- The crock itself can double up as a serving dish if you want to take it to the table.
- A slow cooker is safe to be left unattended.
- You can prepare very healthy meals as the recipes do not require any oil or fat.

TIPS FOR SUCCESSFUL SLOW COOKING

- Always cook for the allotted time.
- Never lift the lid or disturb or stir the contents during the cooking time unless instructed.
- If the food is not cooked at the end of the allotted time, turn the heat to HIGH and cook for a further hour.
- Fill the slow cooker one-half to two-thirds full. If you fill it right up to the top the ingredients will not cook properly.
- Always try to cut your ingredients into similar-sized pieces so that they all cook at the same rate.
- If you like a richer gravy, brown the meat first for about 5–10 minutes in a frying pan.
- Ingredients such as onions can be softened for 5 minutes in a frying pan before adding.
- Do not put frozen foods in a slow cooker – make sure they are thoroughly defrosted first.
- Foods that are on the base of the slow cooker will cook faster because they are immersed in the cooking liquid.
- Always remove skin from poultry and trim off any excess fat from meat. During the long cooking times, the fat will melt and give an unpleasant flavour to the dish.
- If you want to thicken a sauce and heighten the flavour, cook the ingredients on HIGH for the last half hour of cooking time, without the lid.
- When preparing root vegetables, cut them as

uniformly as possible so that they cook evenly. Root vegetables tend to take longer to cook than meat inside a slow cooker, so place them at the base of the pot.

- Seafood should be added to the crock during the last hour of cooking time otherwise it will become rubbery and inedible. Squid is the only exception.
- If a recipe calls for cayenne pepper or hot Tabasco sauce, add it towards the end of the cooking time as these tend to go bitter if cooked for long periods.
- Vegetables that cook quickly, such as tomatoes and mushrooms, should be added to the crock during the last 45 minutes of cooking time.
- Dairy products should only be added during the last 30 minutes of cooking time, unless the recipe instructs otherwise.
- Spices should only be added to the crock during the last hour of cooking otherwise their flavour will be lost.

ADAPTING CONVENTIONAL RECIPES

Almost any recipe can be adapted for a slow cooker without the necessity to make a great deal of changes. If you are new to this method of cooking, it is a good idea to find a slow-cooker recipe that is as close as possible to the recipe you wish to adapt.

The biggest alteration you will need to make is the amount of liquid added to a recipe. Because the contents of the crock are kept moist by the condensation dripping from the lid it's not necessary to have a lot of liquid at the start of the cooking time. It's advisable to reduce the amount by half and check towards the end of the cooking time to make sure the food is still moist enough; it's easier to add a little more than to take some out.

If you wish to speed up the cooking time, look for a recipe that will allow you to do part of the cooking on the stove top before transferring the ingredients to the crock to finish the cooking.

CONVERTING COOKING TIMES

If you are adapting a conventional recipe for cooking in the slow cooker, follow these guides to gain an idea of how long to cook the ingredients.

TRADITIONAL RECIPE	SLOW COOKER (LOW)	SLOW COOKER (HIGH)
45 minutes	6–10 hours	3–4 hours
50–60 minutes	8–10 hours	4–5 hours

ADDING HERBS AND SPICES

Because of the long, slow cooking time you may have to adjust the types of herbs and spices you would normally cook with.

Using fresh herbs

In traditional cooking, fresh herbs are always considered to be far superior to dried ones, but when it comes to slow cooking they can lose their colour and strength of flavour. Because dried herbs tend to release their flavours gradually, the majority of recipes will suggest the use of these instead of fresh ones. If you prefer to use fresh herbs, don't add them at the beginning – wait until the last 30 minutes of cooking time.

Using spices

Spices are best left whole rather than ground. To enhance their flavour, dry-fry them before putting them inside a muslin bag. If you wish to use ground, it is better to grind your own in a mortar. Some of the hotter spices such as chilli can become bitter if cooked for a long time, so it is advisable to add these towards the end of the cooking time.

ADDING ALCOHOL

If you are using alcohol of any kind you need to remember that it evaporates more slowly than in traditional cooking, resulting in a stronger flavour. Consequently, if you are adapting a recipe for slow cooking, you should reduce the amount of alcohol used by one-third.

USING YOUR SLOW COOKER AS A *BAIN-MARIE*

It might seem impractical at first to cook cakes and puddings in a slow cooker, but in fact it can be done quite easily. You can turn your slow cooker into a *bain-marie* – a French term meaning a hot water bath – by cooking the ingredients in a separate dish that is surrounded by simmering water.

This method of cooking is suitable for pâtés, terrines, custards, cakes and steamed puddings. You will need to have an assortment of dishes that sit conveniently inside the crock, allowing enough space for water to be added so that it comes halfway up the sides of the dish. The dish is placed on an upturned saucer or a trivet so that the water can circulate all around and is covered with kitchen foil to prevent the condensation from the lid dripping directly onto it.

Puddings and cakes cooked in this way remain moist and very light and rice pudding is exceptionally creamy, although it won't have a skin on the surface like the baked variety. You can even make porridge and leave it cooking overnight so that you wake up to a steaming bowl of creamy oatmeal.

Make sure that cake tins are watertight and that they will fit comfortably inside the crock before you fill them with the ingredients. Some recipes require you to line the tin first with greaseproof paper or baking parchment. Remember you cannot use loose-bottomed tins for this method of cooking as they will not be watertight.

PART 2

STOCKS & SAUCES

The basis of many meals is the quality of the stock or sauce, whether it is sweet or savoury. The majority of sauces can be made in a slow cooker with ease and if you want to make a large quantity they can be frozen and used when required.

BROWN MEAT STOCK

A good stock should never be boiled. The slow cooker is ideal, although stocks do benefit from being started in the oven. A *bouquet garni* of parsley, thyme and bay is used in several recipes.

Ask your butcher to chop the beef bones into small, manageable pieces. This will improve the flavour of the stock because the marrowbone jelly will seep out and enrich the liquid.

INGREDIENTS *Makes 4 litres/7 pints*
700g/1lb 8oz beef bones
1 onion, quartered, with skin
1 carrot, sliced
1 celery stick, sliced
8 black peppercorns
6 sprigs of parsley
1 sprig of fresh thyme
2 bay leaves
about 1.2 litres/2 pints cold water

METHOD

1. Preheat the oven to 220°C/ 425°F/gas mark 7.

2. Spread out the bones on a large baking tray and cook in the oven for 15 minutes, turning occasionally. Once the bones are starting to brown, add the vegetables and cook for a further 10 minutes, or until they are just starting to turn brown.

3. Put the bones and vegetables into the crock and add the peppercorns. Using a piece of string, tie the fresh herbs together to make a bouquet garni and drop into the crock.

4. Pour in the cold water, making sure you have sufficient to totally cover the bones. Cover with the lid, turn to HIGH and cook for 2 hours.

5. Skim off any scum from the surface, turn down the heat and cook on LOW for 4–5 hours.

6. Strain the stock through a sieve and chill quickly. Once cold, remove any fat from the surface.

CHICKEN STOCK

This white stock is made using up a chicken carcass and makes a great base for soups and stews using white meat. It can also be used to make the base for a rich gravy to go with roast dinner.

INGREDIENTS *Makes 1 litre/1¾ pints*

1 cooked chicken or turkey carcass
1 onion, roughly chopped
1 leek, roughly chopped
1 celery stick, sliced
1 carrot, sliced
8 white peppercorns
2 sprigs of fresh thyme
2 bay leaves
about 1 litre/1¾ pints cold water

METHOD

1. Break or cut the poultry carcass into manageable pieces so that they will fit comfortably into the slow cooker.

2. Add the prepared vegetables to the crock together with the peppercorns and fresh herbs. Place the carcass pieces on top of the vegetables and add sufficient water to cover everything. Cover with the lid and cook on HIGH for 2 hours.

3. Skim off any surface scum from the stock with a slotted spoon, turn down the heat and cook on LOW for 4 hours.

4. Strain the stock through a fine sieve and chill quickly by placing it over a bowl of ice cubes. Once it is cold, remove any fat that has formed on the surface.

CHEF'S TIP

If you would like to intensify the flavour of any stock, place it in a saucepan and boil rapidly on the stove top until it is reduced by half.

FISH STOCK

This very light stock is made by gently cooking the bones of white fish with the standard stock vegetables. To get a really rich flavour, use the heads and trimmings next time you have fresh prawns.

INGREDIENTS *Makes 900ml/1½ pints*

900g/2lb bones and trimmings from white fish
225g/8oz prawn heads and trimmings
1 onion, roughly sliced
1 celery stick, sliced
1 carrot, sliced
8 white peppercorns
1 *bouquet garni*, made from fresh herbs
about 900ml/1½ pints cold water

METHOD

1. Rinse the fish bones and trimmings and prawn heads and casings.

2. Layer the prepared vegetables in the crock, add the peppercorns and fresh *bouquet garni* and then lay the fish bones and trimmings and prawn heads and casings on top.

3. Pour on sufficient water to cover the contents completely and then cover with the lid. Turn the setting to HIGH and cook for 1 hour.

4. Skim any scum from the surface with a slotted spoon and turn down the heat. Cook on LOW for 1 hour. Make sure you do not cook it for longer than the recommended time otherwise the stock will become bitter and unpleasant.

5. Pour the stock through a fine sieve and cool quickly. Cover with cling film and store in the refrigerator for up to 4 days, or freeze it for later use.

VEGETABLE STOCK

When making this stock choose vegetables that are really fresh. Avoid using potatoes as they contain a lot of starch which will produce a cloudy rather than a clear broth.

INGREDIENTS *Makes 1.2 litres/2 pints*

1 large onion, roughly chopped
1 leek, sliced
2 carrots, sliced
2 celery sticks, sliced
115g/4oz butternut squash, peeled and diced
2 bay leaves
1 sprig of fresh thyme
1 sprig of fresh oregano
1 sprig of fresh parsley
8 whole white peppercorns
about 1.2 litre/2 pints cold water

METHOD

1. Prepare all the vegetables. Put all the ingredients into the slow cooker and cover with the lid. Turn the heat to HIGH and cook for 2 hours.

2. Skim off any scum from the surface of the stock using a slotted spoon and turn down the heat. Cook on LOW for a further 2 hours.

3. Strain the stock through a fine sieve and cool rapidly. Store in the refrigerator for up to 5 days or freeze for later use.

CHEF'S TIP

To make your own stock cubes out of any of the recipes given here, simply reduce the stock by boiling on the stove top until the liquid has reduced by half. Leave it to cool and then pour into ice cube trays and place in the freezer until you are ready to use them.

CLASSIC TOMATO SAUCE

Tomato sauce is the base for many recipes, particularly pasta dishes, so it's a good idea to make a large batch and freeze it so that you always have some handy.

INGREDIENTS *Makes 500ml/16fl oz*

1 tbsp olive oil
1 onion, finely chopped
2 garlic cloves, finely chopped
900g/2lb ripe tomatoes, roughly chopped
1 red pepper, deseeded and roughly chopped
2 celery sticks, finely chopped
150g/5½oz tomato purée
2 tbsp red wine
1 tsp dried basil
1 tsp dried thyme
1 tsp dried oregano
½ tsp salt
½ tsp freshly ground black pepper
1 tsp caster sugar
1 tsp dried chilli flakes
10 button mushrooms, quartered

METHOD

1. Pour the olive oil in the base of the crock and add the finely chopped onion and garlic. Stir to coat the onion and garlic in oil, cover with the lid and then set the cooker to HIGH. Cook for 15 minutes.

2. Add the tomatoes, pepper and celery to the crock, followed by the tomato purée, wine, dried basil, thyme, oregano, salt, pepper and sugar. Stir to combine and then cover with the lid and cook on LOW for 3 hours.

3. After 2½ hours, carefully remove the lid and test to see if the celery and other vegetables are tender. If you are happy with the consistency, stir in the chilli flakes and mushrooms and continue to cook on LOW for the final 30 minutes. Test for seasoning and either cool and freeze or use as required.

WHITE SAUCE

A traditional white sauce needs to be watched continually through the cooking process, otherwise it can burn or go lumpy. Made in the slow cooker, it can be left – giving you time to do other things!

INGREDIENTS *Makes 500ml/16fl oz*

400ml/14fl oz semi-skimmed or whole milk
2 bay leaves
½ onion, finely chopped
6 black peppercorns
1 cinnamon stick
30g/1oz butter, softened
30g/1oz plain flour
1 tsp dry mustard powder
salt and pepper to taste

METHOD

1. Pour the milk into the crock and add the bay leaves, onion, peppercorns and cinnamon stick. Put the lid on the cooker, switch the setting to HIGH and leave for 1 hour or until the liquid is simmering.

2. Remove the lid and take out the ingredients used for flavouring with a slotted spoon.

3. In a small bowl, combine the butter, flour and mustard powder to form a smooth paste. Add a little of the hot milk from the crock and whisk until it is smooth and thoroughly combined.

4. Pour the flour paste into the crock and whisk into the hot milk until the mixture has thickened nicely.

5. Put on the lid and cook for 30 minutes on HIGH. You can make an exception to the rule with this recipe and lift the lid from time to time in order to stir the sauce to make sure that it isn't going lumpy.

6. Test for seasoning at the end of the cooking time and add salt and pepper to taste.

SAUCES FOR FONDUE

If you don't have a special fondue set it needn't stop you from enjoying this special treat – simply use your slow cooker and make one of these delicious dips.

CHEESE FONDUE

INGREDIENTS *Serves 6–8*

150ml/5 fl oz dry white wine
2 garlic cloves, minced
225g/8oz gruyère cheese, grated
225g/8oz smoked Swiss cheese, grated
2 tsp cornflour
½ tsp hot smoked paprika

METHOD

1. Reserve 1 tbsp of the wine. Put the remainder of the wine in a saucepan with the garlic and bring to a simmer. Add the two cheeses and stir until melted.

2. In a small bowl, mix the cornflour with the reserved tablespoon of wine until you have a paste. Gradually mix this into the wine and cheese in the saucepan and stir briskly until the mixture starts to thicken.

3. Pour the cheese mixture into your slow cooker and turn the setting to LOW. Cover with a lid and cook for 1 hour.

4. Remove the lid, give the sauce a good stir and then replace the cover and cook for an additional 2 hours until the mixture has heated through thoroughly.

5. Just before serving, sprinkle the top with the smoked paprika and serve immediately, leaving the cheese sauce in the crock.

SUGGESTED DIPPERS

Chunks of fresh bread, broccoli and cauliflower florets, sweet pepper, sweet apples or carrot sticks.

BUTTERSCOTCH FONDUE

INGREDIENTS *Serves 4–6*

115g/4oz unsalted butter, cubed
115g/4oz dark brown sugar
200ml/7fl oz double cream
1 vanilla pod, seeds only
2–3 tsp dark rum

METHOD

1. Put the butter into the crock and add the sugar. Heat on HIGH without a lid for about 15 minutes, or until you see the butter starting to melt.
2. Pour in the cream and keep stirring until the sugar has dissolved.
3. Split the vanilla pod and remove the seeds using the blade of a knife. Drop the seeds into the crock together with the rum. Cover with the lid and cook on HIGH for 30 minutes, stirring occasionally, until the sauce is thick and creamy.
4. Once it is at the desired consistency, turn the heat to LOW. It can be kept warm for up to 1 hour before serving.
5. When you are ready to serve, turn off the slow cooker and put the crock on the table. As the sauce starts to cool it will thicken slightly and adhere to the fruit dippers.

SUGGESTED DIPPERS

Any fresh fruits, peeled and cut into handy-sized sticks: pieces of banana, marshmallows, strips of plain cake such as Madeira or Victoria sponge, vanilla wafers or biscotti.

If you are using this fondue for a children's party, omit the rum and make some fun shapes out of pieces of cake that you can put on the end of lolly sticks or wooden skewers. This fondue also works very well drizzled over vanilla ice cream for a really special treat.

BARBECUE SAUCE

Try this delicious sauce spread on barbecued spareribs.

INGREDIENTS *Makes 360ml/12fl oz*

200ml/7fl oz tomato ketchup
1 tbsp Worcestershire sauce
1 tsp hot chilli sauce
200ml/7fl oz water
60ml/2fl oz malt vinegar
1 tbsp brown sugar
1 tsp salt
1 tsp dry mustard powder
1 tsp celery seed
60g/2oz onion, finely chopped

METHOD

Combine all the above ingredients in the crock of your slow cooker, cover with the lid and cook on LOW for 2–3 hours. Store in sterilized bottles.

CRANBERRY & APPLE SAUCE

This makes a nice change from traditional apple sauce next time you serve roast pork.

INGREDIENTS *makes 200g/7oz*

100g/3½oz fresh cranberries
2 cooking apples, peeled, cored and chopped
115g/4oz sugar
1 cinnamon stick
6 whole cloves
½ nutmeg

METHOD

Put the cranberries, apples and sugar in the crock of your slow cooker. Put the spices in a muslin square and tie with a piece of string. Add to the crock, cover with the lid and cook on LOW for 4–5 hours or until the fruit is soft.

CHOCOLATE SAUCE

This rich, velvety sauce is perfect to turn ordinary puddings into something really special. You can choose between a creamy or dark chocolate according to your taste.

FOR A CREAMY SAUCE

INGREDIENTS *Makes 250ml/8fl oz*

200ml/7fl oz double cream
60ml/2fl oz semi-skimmed milk
1 vanilla pod, seeds only
150g/5½oz dark chocolate (80% cocoa), broken into small pieces

METHOD

1. Pour the cream and milk into the crock.

2. Split the vanilla pod and scrape out the seeds using the blade of a knife. Add the seeds to the crock. Turn the cooker to HIGH and cook, uncovered, for about 45 minutes.

3. Turn the slow cooker off and add the chocolate pieces. Stir continuously until all the chocolate has melted. Serve the sauce while it is still warm.

FOR A DARK, GLOSSY SAUCE

INGREDIENTS *Makes 250ml/8fl oz*

225g/8oz dark chocolate (80% cocoa), broken into small pieces
4 tbsp golden syrup
30g/1oz unsalted butter, diced and softened

METHOD

Put all the ingredients into the crock and turn the setting to HIGH. Cook, uncovered, for about 30 minutes, stirring frequently, until the chocolate has melted. Serve warm. This is perfect spooned over profiteroles.

FRUIT PURÉE

In the slow cooker, soft fruits retain their flavour and you don't risk overcooking them. Pour fruit purées over ice cream, use as a base for steamed puddings or spoon over baked apples.

INGREDIENTS *Makes 360ml/12fl oz*

350g/12oz fresh apricots, blackberries, blackcurrants, blueberries, cherries, plums, raspberries or strawberries
3 tbsp water
100g/3½oz sugar (or to taste)
grated zest of ½ lemon or orange
1 tsp vanilla essence

METHOD

1. If you are cooking cherries, plums, apricots or similar stoned fruits you will need to cut them in half, remove the pit and then chop the flesh into small pieces. Prepare the fruit by washing it and removing any hulls or stalks.

2. Put all the ingredients into the crock and give them a stir until the sugar starts to dissolve. Cover with the lid and cook on HIGH for 1–1½ hours, or until the fruit is really soft.

3. When you are happy that the fruit is cooked, pour the mixture into a food processor and blend until you have a smooth purée. Test for sweetness at this stage and add extra sugar if necessary.

4. To get rid of any pips or pieces of peel, press the purée through a fine sieve, discarding anything that doesn't go through.

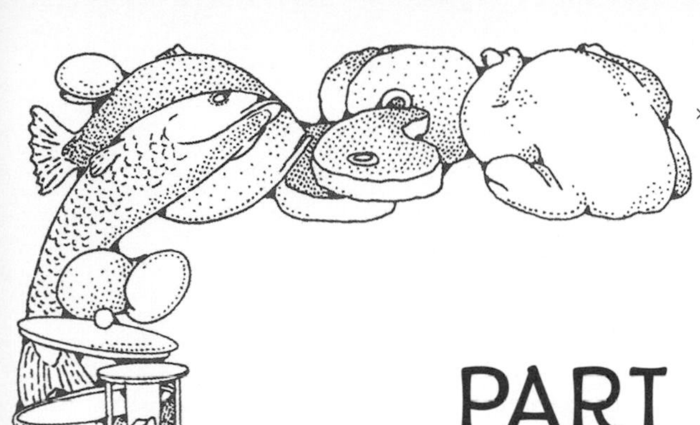

PART 3

SOUPS & APPETIZERS

The slow cooker is particularly suitable for making soups because the long, slow cooking time means that all the flavours have time to develop, giving the final dish a really rich, full flavour. Pâtés and terrines can also be easily adapted for cooking in the slow cooker.

MAKING SOUPS

The joy of making soups is that although the preparation takes a while, once all the ingredients are added to the slow cooker they can be left to cook and form a rich broth.

There's no limit to the number or variety of vegetables that you can use to make a soup, but make sure you only choose really fresh produce to get the best flavour. If you grow your own vegetables you will probably find that you make seasonal soups, using vegetables that are available at that time of year.

If you are using onions in a soup recipe, it is advisable to fry them on the hob first, as they take longer to cook than any other vegetable. Browning them first also means the soup will have a richer flavour once cooked.

All soups benefit from long, slow cooking so you needn't worry if you are out for the day and can't get back to turn the slow cooker off – the soup won't spoil from a couple of hours extra cooking.

A soup relies on a good stock as a base, so you should use some of the stocks made in Part 1 of this book. If you have plenty of stocks in reserve you will always be able to make a soup of some kind, even if you have to substitute other ingredients.

You can use either dry or fresh herbs, but they need to be treated in different ways. Dried ones can be added at the beginning of the recipe, whereas the amount of fresh herbs used should be double the quantity of dried and only added at the end of the cooking period.

If you want to make a soup that includes meat, add it at the start of a recipe and cook for 1 hour on HIGH before turning the setting down to LOW for the remaining time.

BUTTERNUT SQUASH & GINGER SOUP

Butternut squash has beautiful orange flesh which does not lose its colour when cooked. Blended with ginger and spices, it makes an irresistible soup.

INGREDIENTS *Serves 4*

1 butternut squash
2 tbsp olive oil
2 onions, finely chopped
750ml/1¼ pints vegetable stock (see p.23)
2 eating apples, peeled, cored and diced
5cm/2in fresh root ginger, peeled and grated
salt and freshly ground black pepper
½ tsp grated nutmeg
½ tsp ground cloves
½ tsp ground coriander
½ tsp ground cinnamon
1 tsp hot smoked paprika
sour cream, to serve

METHOD

1. Preheat the oven to 200°C/400°F/gas mark 6.

2. Cut the butternut squash in half, scrape out the seeds and stringy pulp and then brush the inside with the olive oil. Place the halves skin-side down on a roasting tray and bake in the oven for about 20 minutes or until you can easily remove the rind from the flesh.

3. Put the flesh of the squash in the crock of your slow cooker with the remaining ingredients except for the sour cream, cover with a lid and cook on LOW for 6–8 hours.

4. Blend the soup in batches until you have a smooth consistency, then put into a large saucepan and reheat. Taste for seasoning and when you are ready to serve, pour it into warmed bowls and swirl a little sour cream over the surface of each bowl to make an attractive pattern.

CABBAGE & SMOKED SAUSAGE SOUP

This hearty soup will be loved by all the family, and your children probably won't even notice they are eating vegetables!

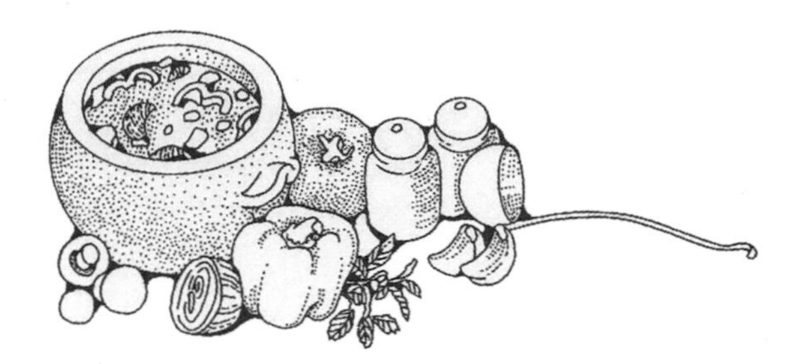

INGREDIENTS *Serves 6*

1 tbsp olive oil
1 onion, finely chopped
1 small cabbage, finely shredded
400g/14oz can cannellini beans, drained
450g/1lb smoked sausage, sliced
1 tsp dried rosemary
1 tsp dried thyme
1.5 litres/2¾ pints vegetable stock (see p.23)
salt and freshly ground black pepper, to taste

METHOD

1. Heat the oil in a frying pan and fry the onion until lightly browned. Add this to the crock of your slow cooker, along with the cabbage, cannellini beans, smoked sausage and dried herbs.

2. Heat the vegetable stock to boiling point and pour over the ingredients in the crock. Cover with a lid and cook on HIGH for 1 hour.

3. Turn the setting to LOW and cook for a further 3 hours or until the vegetables are soft.

4. Check the seasoning and add salt and black pepper to taste. Serve piping hot with some crusty bread.

CARROT & CORIANDER SOUP

The natural sweetness of carrots comes out when they are cooked slowly. Partnered with coriander, they make a fragrant soup.

INGREDIENTS *Serves 4*

1 tbsp olive oil
45g/1½oz unsalted butter
1 onion, finely chopped
1 celery stick, chopped
2 medium-sized potatoes, peeled and chopped
450g/1lb carrots, chopped
900ml/1½ pints vegetable stock (see p.23)
2 tsp ground coriander
salt and freshly ground black pepper
1 tbsp chopped fresh coriander
150ml/5fl oz whole milk or double cream
fresh watercress, to garnish

METHOD

1. Heat the oil and butter in a large frying pan and sauté the onions until softened, but do not allow them to go brown. Add the chopped celery and potato and cook for a further 2 minutes. Add the carrot and cook for 1 more minute. Transfer all the sautéed vegetables to the crock of your slow cooker.

2. Put the vegetable stock into a saucepan and bring to the boil. Pour the boiling stock over the top of the vegetables in the crock. Add the ground coriander and season with a little salt and pepper. Cover the crock with the lid and cook on LOW for 4–5 hours, or until the vegetables are tender.

3. Ladle the soup into a blender and blend until you have a smooth purée. Pour the soup into a saucepan, add the chopped fresh coriander and the milk (or cream), stir and heat until piping hot. Check the seasoning and serve garnished with watercress.

CHICKEN NOODLE SOUP

Chicken noodle soup is always a family favourite and can be made simply in a slow cooker.

INGREDIENTS *Serves 8*

30g/1oz unsalted butter
2 onions, sliced
2 carrots, sliced
2 celery sticks, cut into 2.5cm/1in slices
1 whole chicken (about 1.8kg/4lb in weight)
1 tsp salt
½ tsp freshly ground black pepper
½ tsp dried basil
120ml/4fl oz white wine
2 litres/3½ pints chicken stock (see p.21)
175g/6oz fine egg noodles

METHOD

1. Heat the butter in a frying pan and add the onions. Cook over a medium heat until softened but do not allow them to brown.
2. Place the onion in the crock of your slow cooker and add the carrots and celery. Place the whole chicken on top of the vegetables and season with salt and pepper and the dried basil.
3. Pour in the white wine, cover with the lid and cook on LOW for 8–10 hours or until the chicken is starting to fall off the bone.
4. When the chicken is cooked, remove the meat and vegetables, place in a bowl and set aside.
5. Transfer the juices into a large saucepan and stir in the chicken stock. Bring to the boil and add the noodles. Cook for 10 minutes, or until the noodles are tender.
6. Remove the meat from the chicken carcass and shred. Discard the bones and skin and then add the chicken meat and vegetables to the saucepan. Cook for 2 minutes and then spoon into bowls while it is still piping hot.

CHILLED SWEET PEPPER SOUP

This chilled soup is perfect for a hot summer's day, served with crème fraîche and crusty bread.

INGREDIENTS *Serves 4*

6 sweet red peppers
2 tbsp olive oil
1 onion, finely chopped
2 garlic cloves, finely chopped
300g/10oz ripe tomatoes, skinned and roughly chopped
120ml/4fl oz red wine
400ml/14fl oz vegetable stock (see p.23)
1 tsp caster sugar
1 tsp dried thyme
1 tsp hot smoked paprika
salt and freshly ground black pepper
chopped fresh chives, to garnish
brown breadcrumbs mixed with dried chillies, to garnish

METHOD

1. Cut the peppers into quarters, remove the seeds and veins and then place them on baking trays, skin-side up, under a hot grill. Grill until the skins start to char and blister, then put the peppers in a bowl and cover with a plate.

2. Heat the oil in a frying pan and gently cook the onion and garlic for 10 minutes until they are soft but not browned.

3. While the onion is cooking, peel the skin from the peppers and roughly chop the flesh.

4. Put the peppers, tomatoes, onion and garlic into the crock with the remaining ingredients except the garnish.

5. Cover with a lid and cook on HIGH for 3–4 hours or until all the vegetables are tender. Leave to cool for 10 minutes then transfer to a blender and blend until smooth.

6. Serve the soup chilled with chopped chives and a sprinkling of brown breadcrumbs mixed with dried chillies.

CLAM & POTATO CHOWDER

A chowder is very similar to soup, but it is thick and a meal in itself, especially if served with chunks of fresh French bread.

INGREDIENTS *Serves 4*

30g/1oz unsalted butter
2 rashers of smoked bacon, finely chopped
1 onion, finely chopped
4 ×175g/6oz cans clams with juice
6 medium-sized potatoes, peeled and diced
750ml/1¼ pints water
2 tsp salt
½ tsp freshly ground black pepper
3 tbsp cornflour
750ml/1¼ pints whole milk (or half milk and half single cream)
chopped fresh parsley, to garnish

METHOD

1. Heat the butter in a frying pan and fry the bacon and onion until they are nicely browned.

2. Put the clams (either whole or chopped into small pieces) and their juice into the crock of your slow cooker. Add the onion and bacon, potatoes, water and salt and pepper. Cover with the lid and cook on HIGH for 3–4 hours or until the vegetables are tender.

3. During the last hour of cooking, combine the cornflour with a little of the milk (or milk and cream) until it is thoroughly blended into a paste. Add this mixture to the slow cooker together with the remaining milk and stir well to combine. Continue to cook on HIGH until the chowder has thickened nicely.

4. Serve the chowder piping hot in bowls, topped with some chopped fresh parsley.

CREAM OF SPINACH SOUP

This nutritious soup is an amazing bright green colour which is achieved by keeping some of the spinach back from the slow cooker and adding it just before serving.

INGREDIENTS *Serves 4*

30g/1oz unsalted butter
1 medium onion, finely chopped
2 garlic cloves, finely chopped
1 medium potato, peeled and diced
450ml/15fl oz vegetable stock (see p.23)
600ml/1 pint milk
450g/1lb fresh spinach, washed and roughly chopped
zest of ½ lemon, finely grated
1 tsp freshly grated nutmeg
salt and freshly ground black pepper
3 tbsp double cream, to serve

METHOD

1. Heat the butter in a frying pan and fry the onion and garlic for 5–6 minutes over medium heat until they are softened but not browned. Stir in the potato and continue to cook gently for 1 more minute. Put the onion and potato mixture into the crock of your slow cooker.

2. Add the vegetable stock, milk, two-thirds of the spinach, the lemon zest and grated nutmeg. Cover with the lid and cook on LOW for 6–8 hours, or until the vegetables are tender.

3. Allow the soup to cool slightly and then put it in a blender with the remaining spinach. Blend until it is silky smooth.

4. Reheat the soup in a saucepan, season to taste with salt and pepper and then serve in bowls with the cream swirled on the top.

CREAMY CELERY SOUP

Celery is an underrated vegetable, but if eaten during the winter months when it is at its best it makes an aromatic and filling soup.

INGREDIENTS *Serves 4–6*

1 tbsp olive oil
45g/1½oz unsalted butter
1 large onion, finely chopped
2 garlic cloves, finely chopped
1 large potato, peeled and cut into small dice
10 celery sticks, sliced
1 fennel bulb, trimmed, cored and chopped
900ml/1½ pints hot vegetable stock (see p.23)
1 tsp celery salt
freshly ground black pepper
2 tbsp double cream
1 tsp hot smoked paprika
celery leaves, to garnish

METHOD

1. Heat the oil and butter in a large frying pan and cook the onion over a medium heat until translucent. Add the garlic and cook for a further minute. Add the potato, celery and fennel and cook for 2 minutes.

2. Put all the fried vegetables into the crock of your slow cooker. Heat the stock to boiling point and pour over the top of the vegetables. Season with the celery salt and black pepper, cover with the lid and cook on LOW for 4–5 hours or until the vegetables are tender.

3. Once the vegetables are cooked, transfer the soup to a blender and blend until you have a smooth purée. Pour the soup into a saucepan, check the seasoning and add the double cream. Heat the soup thoroughly before serving but do not allow it to come to the boil as this can curdle the cream.

4. Serve in bowls sprinkled with the paprika and some chopped celery leaves.

FRENCH ONION SOUP

You lose none of the traditional flavour of this classic soup by cooking it in a slow cooker and you can still top it with your favourite cheesy croutons.

INGREDIENTS *Serves 4*

30g/1oz unsalted butter
2 tsp olive oil
1.1kg/2½lb onions, sliced
1 tsp caster sugar
1 tbsp plain flour
1 tbsp brandy
1 litre/1¾ pints brown meat stock (see p.20)
1 tsp dried thyme
salt and freshly ground black pepper

FOR THE CHEESY CROUTONS:
4 slices of French bread or ciabatta
1 garlic clove, halved
60g/2oz grated gruyère

METHOD

1. Heat the butter and olive oil in a large frying pan and fry the onions until they are soft and starting to go brown. Add the sugar and continue to cook the onions until they are golden brown.

2. Put the onions into the crock of your slow cooker and sprinkle the flour over. Add the brandy, meat stock and dried thyme and stir until thoroughly combined. Cover with the lid and cook on HIGH for 2 hours or until the onions are very soft. Season with salt and pepper.

3. To make the cheesy bread, put the bread slices under a low grill until they start to go dry and slightly brown. Rub them all over with the cut surface of the garlic and then sprinkle the grated cheese over them.

4. Pour the soup into 4 flameproof bowls, top with the cheesy croutons and put under a hot grill until the cheese has melted.

LEEK, POTATO & WATERCRESS SOUP

When there's a nip in the air and the leeks are standing proud in the ground it is time to make this hearty soup.

INGREDIENTS *Serves 4*
3 leeks, sliced
1 onion, sliced
1 large shallot, sliced
3 large potatoes, peeled and diced
60g/2oz watercress, stalks removed
1 tsp dried thyme
1 tsp dried oregano
200ml/7fl oz apple juice
1 litre/1¾ pints vegetable stock (see p.23)
150ml/5fl oz double cream
salt and freshly ground black pepper
chopped fresh parsley, to garnish

METHOD

1. Put all the vegetables in the crock of your slow cooker and add the thyme and oregano. Pour in the apple juice and vegetable stock. Cover with the lid and cook on HIGH for 2 hours, then turn down the heat to LOW and cook for a further 6 hours or until all the vegetables are tender.

2. Pour the soup into a blender and blend until smooth or, alternatively, use a hand blender. If you like a chunkier soup, don't blend the whole batch so that you still have some pieces of potato and leek.

3. Put the soup into a large saucepan, bring to the boil, then turn down the heat and add the cream. Season with salt and pepper to taste. Do not allow the mixture to come to the boil once you have added the cream otherwise you risk it curdling.

4. Serve the soup piping hot with a sprinkling of chopped fresh parsley as a garnish.

MINESTRONE SOUP

This is the perfect soup to eat in front of the fire on a cold winter's night with some crunchy garlic bread.

INGREDIENTS *Serves 4*

30g/1oz unsalted butter
60g/2oz streaky bacon, chopped
1 large onion, finely chopped
1 garlic clove, finely chopped
3 celery sticks, chopped
300g/10oz peeled and diced potato (prepared weight)
2 carrots, diced
¼ cabbage, shredded
3 tomatoes, skinned and roughly chopped
1.2 litres/2 pints vegetable stock (see p.23)
1 tbsp tomato purée
1 tsp sweet paprika
1 tbsp Worcestershire sauce
salt and freshly ground black pepper, to taste
2 tbsp chopped fresh parsley
75g/2½oz small pasta shells
freshly grated Parmesan cheese, to garnish

METHOD

1. Melt the butter in a frying pan over a medium heat and fry the bacon and vegetables until they are starting to go soft. Tip into the crock of your slow cooker.

2. Add the stock and the remaining ingredients with the exception of the fresh parsley, pasta shells and Parmesan cheese. Cover with the lid and cook on LOW for 4–6 hours. At the beginning of the last hour of cooking time, add the chopped parsley and the pasta shells. Give the soup a stir, add a little more seasoning if necessary and then cover and leave for the last hour to finish cooking.

3. When you are ready to serve, spoon the soup into bowls and sprinkle the surface with a good helping of Parmesan cheese.

MIXED MUSHROOM SOUP

Mushroom soup has a unique earthy flavour, especially if you use a mixture of fresh varieties as well as a few dried ones for intensity.

INGREDIENTS *Serves 4*

30g/1oz dried porcini mushrooms
600ml/1 pint chicken stock (see p.21)
30g/1oz unsalted butter
1 onion, finely chopped
2 garlic cloves, finely chopped
450g/1lb mixed mushrooms such as ceps, button mushrooms, chanterelles, oyster
1 tbsp plain flour
½ tsp dried thyme
60ml/2fl oz dry sherry
salt and freshly ground black pepper, to taste
60ml/2fl oz sour cream
chopped fresh parsley, to garnish

METHOD

1. Put the dried mushrooms in the crock of your slow cooker. Heat the chicken stock to near boiling point and pour half the quantity over the mushrooms. Cover with the lid and turn the setting to HIGH.

2. Melt the butter in a frying pan, add the onion and cook for 5–6 minutes or until it is golden brown. Add the garlic and fresh mushrooms and cook for a further 3–4 minutes. Sprinkle the flour over the mushrooms in the pan and add the dried thyme.

Cook for 3 minutes, stirring constantly, until the ingredients are well mixed and the flour is cooked.

3. Stir in the dry sherry and the remaining stock. Season with salt and pepper to taste and bring to the boil.

4. Transfer the contents of the frying pan to the slow cooker. Cook for 1 hour, covered, then turn down to LOW and cook for a further 3–4 hours, or until the mushrooms are tender.

5. Leave the soup to cool for 15 minutes, then ladle into a blender. Blend until it is smooth and strain through a fine nylon sieve into a clean saucepan, carefully pressing any pieces left in the sieve with the back of a spoon.

6. When you are ready to serve, reheat the soup, then stir in half the amount of sour cream.

7. Serve the soup in warmed bowls. Swirl the remaining sour cream over the top and garnish with chopped fresh parsley. Alternatively, serve with herby garlic croûtons (right).

HERBY GARLIC CROÛTONS

3 tbsp olive oil
4 garlic cloves, minced
1 tsp dried basil
1 tsp dried oregano
200g/7oz day-old bread, cubed
grated Parmesan cheese
salt and pepper

METHOD

Preheat the oven to 180°C/350°F/gas mark 4. Heat the oil in a frying pan, add the garlic and herbs and cook over medium heat for 2 minutes. Remove the pan from the heat and toss the bread cubes until they are thoroughly coated. Season with salt and pepper, place the bread on a baking tray covered with baking parchment and sprinkle with Parmesan. Bake for 30 minutes until golden brown.

OXTAIL SOUP

Because oxtail takes a long time to cook to release all of its flavours, the slow cooker is the perfect choice for this soup.

INGREDIENTS *Serves 6*

1 oxtail
2 carrots, sliced
1 onion, sliced
2 celery sticks, sliced
1 *bouquet garni*
salt and freshly ground black pepper
2 tsp cornflour
2 tsp lemon juice
chopped fresh parsley, to garnish

METHOD

1. Remove any excess fat from the oxtail, then divide into joints.
2. Put the prepared vegetables in the crock of your slow cooker with the bouquet garni and season with salt and pepper.
3. Lay the oxtail pieces on top of the vegetables and fill the crock three-quarters full with cold water. Cover and cook on LOW heat for 8–10 hours or until the meat of the oxtail is falling off the bone. Remove the oxtail from the crock and allow to cool. Once it is cold enough to handle, take the meat off the bones and set aside.
4. Pour the soup into a large bowl, discarding the *bouquet garni*, and chill in the refrigerator. Remove any fat from the surface with a slotted spoon.
5. Blend the cornflour with a little of the cold soup.
6. Pour the soup into a large saucepan and add the cornflour mixture. Bring to the boil, stirring until the soup has thickened.
7. Add the meat from the oxtail to the soup, together with the lemon juice. Test for seasoning. Bring back to boiling point and serve it while still piping hot with chopped parsley on top.

TOMATO & BASIL SOUP

An all-time favourite, tomato soup is the stuff of childhood memories. Use tomatoes when they are ripe and sweet from the vine.

INGREDIENTS *Serves 4*

30g/1oz unsalted butter
1 tbsp olive oil
1 onion, finely chopped
1 garlic clove, finely chopped
900g/2lb ripe tomatoes, skinned and roughly chopped
1 red chilli, deseeded and finely chopped
120ml/4fl oz dry white wine
600ml/1 pint vegetable stock (see p.23)
2 tbsp sun-dried tomato purée
1 tsp caster sugar
2 tbsp roughly torn fresh basil
150ml/5fl oz double cream
salt and freshly ground black pepper
whole basil leaves, to garnish

METHOD

1. Heat the butter and olive oil in a saucepan and fry the onion gently for 5 minutes, stirring, until it is soft but not brown.

2. Add the garlic, tomatoes and chilli to the pan. Cover with the wine and vegetable stock and bring to the boil.

3. Pour the tomato mixture into the crock of your slow cooker, add the sun-dried tomato purée and sugar and cover with the lid. Cook on HIGH for 1 hour, then reduce the setting to LOW and cook for a further 4–6 hours to allow all the flavours to blend.

4. Transfer the soup to a blender (or use a hand blender) and blend until it is smooth. Pour the soup into a large saucepan and add the shredded basil and the cream. Season with salt and pepper to taste and heat through, but do not allow it to boil.

5. Serve immediately in warmed bowls garnished with whole basil leaves.

COUNTRY-STYLE TERRINE

This is a type of meatloaf made in the slow cooker that provides a tasty hors d'oeuvre or a great addition to any picnic.

INGREDIENTS *Serves 6–8*

85g/3oz pancetta
2 onions, quartered
1 garlic clove, finely chopped
450g/1lb minced pork
450g/1lb minced veal
2 tbsp dry sherry
60g/2oz ground pistachio nuts
1 tsp black peppercorns
1 tsp salt
1 tsp dried thyme
¼ tsp ground allspice
4 bay leaves

METHOD

1. Put the pancetta, onions and garlic into a food processor and process until finely chopped.

2. Put the pancetta mixture into a large bowl with the pork, veal, sherry, pistachios, salt, thyme and allspice and mix together, using your hands.

3. Lay the bay leaves in a loaf tin that will fit inside your slow cooker (about 20 × 12.5cm/8 × 5in). Spread the meat mixture evenly in the loaf tin, cover with kitchen foil and secure with a piece of string. Stand the tin inside the crock of your slow cooker on a trivet or upturned saucer, then pour in enough boiling water to come halfway up the loaf tin. Cover with the lid and cook on HIGH for 3 hours or until the interior temperature reaches 80°C/170°F.

4. Remove the tin from the slow cooker but do not remove the foil. Cool, then place a heavy weight on top and leave the terrine in the fridge overnight for the flavours to develop. To remove the terrine from the mould, dip the tin in hot water, run a sharp knife around the inside and then invert onto a serving plate.

MUSHROOM & CHICKEN PÂTÉ

Very easily made in the slow cooker, this is a delicious appetizer that works well on lightly toasted bread or crackers.

INGREDIENTS *Serves 8*

3 rashers of streaky bacon, cut into small pieces
60g/2oz plain flour
1 tsp salt
½ tsp ground black pepper
450g/1lb chicken livers, cut into small pieces
450g/1lb mushrooms, finely chopped
450ml/15fl oz chicken stock (see p.21)
2 tbsp dry white wine

METHOD

1. Dry fry the bacon in a frying pan until crisp and then drain on a piece of kitchen paper.

2. Mix the flour, salt and pepper in a large freezer bag, add the chopped chicken liver and seal the bag. Shake vigorously to coat all the liver in flour.

3. Fry the chicken liver in the frying pan containing the fat from the bacon until it is nicely browned – this should take 5–6 minutes. Add the chopped mushrooms and cook for another couple of minutes or until the mushrooms are soft. Add half the chicken stock and all of the wine and mix until well combined. Bring to the boil and then pour into the crock of a slow cooker.

4. Crumble the bacon into the crock and stir in the remainder of the stock. Cover with a lid and cook on LOW for 3 hours. If you find the mixture is looking a little too dry towards the end of the cooking time, add a little more chicken stock and stir to combine.

5. Line a rectangular cake tin with greaseproof paper. Spoon the pâté into the tin and flatten the surface with a knife. Cool, then refrigerate to solidify.

SMOKED SALMON TERRINE

A light and elegant starter, this combines both fresh and smoked salmon to impress your dinner guests.

INGREDIENTS *Serves 6*

30g/1oz butter, softened
350g/12oz smoked salmon
2 eggs, lightly beaten
100ml/3½fl oz crème fraîche
2 tbsp capers, drained
2 tsp soft pink peppercorns, drained
salt and white pepper
900g/2lb salmon fillets

METHOD

1. Pour about 2.5cm/1in of warm water into the crock of your slow cooker and place an upturned saucer in the base. Turn the slow cooker on to HIGH.

2. Lightly grease a 1 litre/1¾ pint loaf tin with the butter. Use some of the smoked salmon slices to line the tin, allowing them to hang over the sides. Reserve the remaining slices.

3. Combine the eggs, crème fraîche, capers and peppercorns in a bowl and season with salt and pepper. Cut the salmon fillets into small chunks and add to the bowl.

4. Spoon half the fish mixture into the loaf tin and press down with the back of a spoon. Lay the remaining smoked salmon slices over the top, then add the remaining fish mixture, smoothing the surface. Fold the overhanging smoked salmon pieces over the top and cover with a double thickness of foil.

5. Put the tin into the crock and add enough boiling water to come halfway up the sides of the tin. Cook on HIGH for 3–4 hours.

6. When the terrine is ready, place a weight on top, cool, then refrigerate for 24 hours. Turn it out and serve with mayonnaise mixed with fresh dill.

PART 4

FISH & SHELLFISH

Slow cookers are ideal for cooking fish as the slow, moist method of cooking helps to retain the natural, subtle flavour. Smaller fish can be cooked whole, while the larger ones, such as salmon, will need to be cut into fillets or smaller pieces as in the risotto recipe on p.62. Shellfish tend to be added towards the end of the recipe to avoid them becoming overcooked and rubbery in texture.

COOKING FISH

Because it is cooked gently without being disturbed, fish retains its shape and all of its natural flavour in the slow cooker.

There are many different kinds of fish and how they are prepared will depend on the variety you choose and the recipe. Nearly all fish are suitable for cooking in the slow cooker with the exception of live shellfish such as mussels or lobsters as they have to be boiled rapidly and for a very short time.

Unlike vegetable and meat dishes, any recipe containing fish should not be kept warm in the slow cooker after its cooking time as it can dry out. Plan your meal carefully so that you can serve the fish as soon as it has finished cooking.

Poaching is a good way of preparing any type of fish and is very simple to do. The fish is placed in the slow cooker and covered with a liquid such as stock, wine or water, with a few herbs or spices added. If you are cooking very thin fillets in this way, it is a good idea to roll them up first because this helps to keep them moist and really enhances the flavour.

Braising is another method of cooking fish and this involves using a small amount of liquid so that the fish is partly steamed and partly poached. This is a particularly good way of cooking very delicately flavoured fish.

Shellfish can also be cooked in the slow cooker but as long cooking times are not required they are added towards the end. Squid is an exception – this can be added at the beginning as it will withstand longer cooking. Prawns can be cooked in their shells or peeled first; it's advisable to remove the dark intestinal vein if you are using large prawns.

FISH DUMPLINGS IN TOMATO SAUCE

Children love this recipe and it is so easy to prepare and put it on to cook before you pick them up from school.

INGREDIENTS *Serves 4*

400g/14oz tin chopped tomatoes
60g/2oz button mushrooms, chopped
salt and freshly ground black pepper
450g/1lb haddock fillet, skinned and boned
30g/1oz fresh wholemeal breadcrumbs
1 tbsp finely chopped chives
1 tsp dried coriander
2 tbsp chopped spring onions
chopped fresh chives, to garnish

METHOD

1. Put the chopped tomatoes into the crock of your slow cooker and add the mushrooms. Season with a little salt and pepper and then cover with the lid and turn the setting to HIGH. Cook for 2 hours.

2. Make the fish dumplings by cutting the haddock into cubes and placing them in a food processor together with the breadcrumbs, chives and coriander. Process until the fish is finely chopped but still has some texture.

3. Roll the fish mixture into tiny balls (approximately 16) between the palms of your hands. Put them on a plate and keep in the refrigerator until needed.

4. When the tomato sauce has been cooking for 1½ hours, bring the fish balls back to room temperature before adding to the slow cooker. Put them on top of the tomato sauce in a single layer. Cook for 1 hour on HIGH, then reduce the temperature to LOW and cook for a further hour.

5. Serve immediately, piled on top of a plate of steaming spaghetti. Finish the dish by sprinkling the chopped fresh chives over the surface.

FISH CHOWDER

The word 'chowder' has its origins in the Latin word *calderia* – meaning cooking pot – making it a perfect dish for making in the slow cooker.

INGREDIENTS *Serves 4*

1 tbsp olive oil, for greasing
450g/1lb firm white fish fillets, skinned and boned
250g/9oz potatoes, peeled and diced
1 onion, finely chopped
1 celery stick, finely chopped
200g/7oz can sweetcorn
1 tbsp dried parsley
1 tsp dried rosemary
400g/14oz can chopped tomatoes
120ml/4fl oz dry white wine
salt and freshly ground black pepper
3 tbsp plain flour
3 tbsp melted butter
250ml/8fl oz double cream

METHOD

1. Brush the inside of the crock with olive oil and then turn the setting to HIGH.

2. Cut the fish into 2.5cm/1in cubes then place in the slow cooker with the potatoes, onion, celery, sweetcorn, herbs, tomatoes and wine. Season to taste with salt and pepper. Gently stir to combine the ingredients, cover and cook on HIGH for 3 hours.

3. In a bowl, blend the flour with the melted butter and cream and then add to the crock. Mix gently to combine, replace the lid and cook for another hour. Serve immediately.

VARIATIONS

- Add some cooked prawns and a tin of clams when you put in the cream.

GINGER-CITRUS SALMON

Salmon fillets infused with the wonderful flavours of ginger and citrus fruits make a healthy meal when served with crisp stir-fry vegetables.

INGREDIENTS *Serves 4*

4 salmon steaks
120ml/4fl oz water
120ml/4fl oz fresh orange juice
1 red pepper, deseeded and chopped
1 red chilli, deseeded and finely chopped
5cm/2in fresh root ginger, grated
1 lemon, thinly sliced
1 lime, thinly sliced
1 tbsp extra virgin olive oil, plus extra for greasing
salt and freshly ground black pepper
finely chopped fresh coriander and lemon wedges, to garnish

METHOD

1. Brush the inside of the crock of the slow cooker with olive oil and arrange the salmon fillets along the base.

2. In a saucepan, combine the water, orange juice, pepper, chilli and ginger. Bring to a boil over a medium heat.

3. Pour the liquid immediately over the top of the salmon fillets in the crock. Lay the slices of lemon and lime over the top and then drizzle with olive oil. Season with salt and pepper, to taste.

4. Cover with the lid and cook on HIGH for 1½–2 hours or until the salmon is firm to the touch and opaque.

5. To serve, garnish the salmon with chopped coriander and some extra lemon wedges.

JAMBALAYA

This spicy mixture of meat and fish from Louisana developed from the Spanish paella, taking on its own form over the years.

INGREDIENTS *Serves 4*

2 tbsp olive oil
250g/9oz boneless chicken breast, cut into 2.5cm/1in chunks
1 onion, chopped
2 celery sticks, roughly chopped
2 garlic cloves, finely chopped
2 bay leaves
1 tsp dried oregano
½ tsp dried thyme
4 tomatoes, skinned, deseeded and chopped
1 tbsp tomato purée
750ml/1¼ pint fish stock (see p.22)
300g/10oz quick-cook white rice
200g/7oz firm white fish, cubed
salt and freshly ground black pepper
1 tsp cayenne pepper
115g/4oz cooked peeled prawns
8 cooked prawns in their shells and chopped spring onions, to garnish

METHOD

1. Heat the olive oil in a large frying pan and fry the chicken until it is browned on all sides. Reduce the heat, add the onion, celery and garlic and cook for a further 5–10 minutes or until they have softened and started to turn brown.

2. Transfer the chicken and vegetables to the crock of your slow cooker and switch it to HIGH. Add the bay leaves, oregano, thyme, chopped tomatoes and tomato purée.

3. Put the stock in a saucepan and bring to the boil. Pour it immediately over the ingredients in the slow cooker. Stir well to mix the ingredients together, then cover with the lid and cook for 1–1½ hours or until the chicken is tender.

4. Rinse the rice then put in a saucepan with water and bring to the boil. Turn down the heat and simmer for 5 minutes so that it is partially cooked before adding to the crock.

5. Spoon the rice over the top of the ingredients in the crock and then drop the cubes of fish on top. Season with salt and pepper and cayenne pepper and stir to mix the ingredients thoroughly. Cover again and cook for a further 45 minutes on HIGH.

6. Add the prawns, stir, re-cover and cook for a further 15 minutes or until the fish and rice are tender and the majority of the liquid has been absorbed.

7. Serve immediately, garnished with chopped spring onions and whole prawns in their shells on the edge of the plate.

VARIATIONS

- If you would like a spicier version of jambalaya, add a red chilli, deseeded and chopped, when you add the tomatoes.
- Add some cubes of chorizo sausage. Fry it first, though, to remove the excess fat.
- This recipe can be made without the chicken – just double the quantity of fish.

PLAICE ROULADES

You will find this a great dish for a dinner party as these little rolls of fish keep their shape and are moist and delicious.

INGREDIENTS *Serves 4*

4 large plaice fillets, skinned and boned
75g/3oz wholemeal breadcrumbs
60g/2oz almonds, finely chopped
1 tbsp chopped fresh parsley
175g/6oz baby spinach leaves, wilted and drained
2 eggs, lightly beaten
grated zest of ½ lemon
freshly ground black pepper
15g/½oz unsalted butter
120ml/4fl oz dry white wine
8 slices Parma ham

METHOD

1. Wash the fish and pat it dry with some kitchen paper.

2. In a bowl, combine the breadcrumbs, almonds, parsley, spinach, eggs and lemon zest. Season with black pepper and mix together.

3. Rub the inside of the crock with the butter and then add the white wine. Turn the setting to HIGH and while it is heating up prepare the fish.

4. Trim the fat from the Parma ham and then lay 2 slices on top of a piece of cling film, overlapping them.

5. Lay a fish fillet over the top of the ham.

6. Spread a quarter of the filling over the fish fillet and then, starting at the thicker end of the fillet, carefully roll up, using the cling film to pull it together. Seal the ends of the cling film and then place it in the fridge for 15 minutes.

7. Repeat with the other 3 fillets. If you find they unroll when you remove the cling film, secure each one with a cocktail stick.

8. Place the rolls seam-side down in the crock, cover with the lid and cook on LOW for 2 hours.

STUFFED HERRINGS

The juices from these rich, oily fish soak into the stuffing as they cook, making a wonderful supper served with a fresh salad.

INGREDIENTS *Serves 4*

60g/2oz butter
1 onion, finely chopped
75ml/2½fl oz fish stock (see p.22)
60g/2oz fresh wholemeal breadcrumbs
60g/2oz walnuts, roughly chopped
1 tbsp prepared English mustard
finely grated zest and juice of 1 lemon
1 tbsp mixed dried herbs such as chives, parsley, rosemary and thyme
salt and freshly ground black pepper
4 small herrings, heads removed and boned

METHOD

1. Melt half the butter in a frying pan and sauté the onion until it is soft and just starting to go brown.
2. Rub the inside of the crock with the remaining butter, add the fish stock and turn the setting to HIGH.
3. Make the stuffing by mixing together the breadcrumbs, walnuts, mustard, lemon zest, 1 tbsp lemon juice and the mixed herbs. Season to taste. Add the onion and mix together well with your hands.
4. Open up the herrings and stuff the cavities with the filling. Close the herrings and secure with a cocktail stick. With a sharp knife, make 3 deep cuts diagonally across each side of the fish.
5. Lay the fish in the slow cooker and cook on HIGH, covered, for 1½–2 hours or until the fish is cooked. The flesh should come away easily when tested with a fork.
6. Serve immediately, accompanied by a fresh salad.

SWORDFISH STEAKS

Swordfish has a meaty texture and is ideal for cooking in the slow cooker, gently flavoured with dill, lemon and tomatoes.

INGREDIENTS *Serves 4*

2 tbsp olive oil
1 onion, finely sliced
115g/4oz button mushrooms, sliced
1 sweet red pepper, deseeded and chopped
2 tbsp lemon juice
1 tsp dried dill
4 large tomatoes, skinned and roughly chopped
salt and freshly ground black pepper
4 swordfish steaks (about 115g/4oz each)

METHOD

1. Heat the olive oil in a large frying pan and add the chopped onion. Fry gently for 5–6 minutes until soft but not brown. Add the mushrooms, pepper, lemon juice, dill and chopped tomatoes and season with salt and pepper. Cook for a further 3–4 minutes or until the vegetables are just starting to go soft.

2. Wash and dry the swordfish steaks.

3. Place half the tomato mixture in the crock of your slow cooker. Lay the swordfish steaks on top and then finish with the remaining tomato sauce.

4. Turn the setting to HIGH, cover with the lid and cook for 2–3 hours or until the fish is cooked and tender.

5. When the fish is ready, transfer it carefully to warmed serving plates and spoon the sauce over the top. Serve with new potatoes garnished with chopped parsley.

THAI FISH CURRY

Thailand is famous for its fragrant curries and cooking them in a slow cooker gives all the flavours time to infuse.

INGREDIENTS *Serves 4*

1 onion, finely chopped
1 green chilli, deseeded and finely chopped
1 garlic clove, finely chopped
½ tsp fennel seeds
2 tbsp desiccated coconut
150ml/5fl oz water
2 tbsp vegetable oil
¼ tsp cumin seeds
¼ tsp ground coriander
¼ tsp ground cumin
150ml/5fl oz coconut milk
4 cod fillets, skinned and boned
¼ tsp ground turmeric
2 tbsp lime juice
salt, to taste
3 tbsp chopped fresh coriander

METHOD

1. Put the onion, chilli, garlic, fennel seeds and desiccated coconut in a food processor with 2 tablespoons of the water and blend until you have a smooth paste.

2. Heat the oil in a frying pan, add the cumin seeds and fry for 1 minute. Add the paste and fry for 5 minutes. Add the coriander, ground cumin and remaining water and stir to combine. Bring to the boil and cook for 1 minute.

3. Put the mixture into the crock of your slow cooker, add the coconut milk and cook on HIGH, covered, for 1½ hours.

4. Cut the fish into 5cm/2in chunks and marinate in the turmeric, lime juice and salt for 15 minutes.

5. Stir the marinated fish into the crock, cover again and cook for a further 30–40 minutes, or until the fish starts to flake. Stir in the fresh coriander once it is cooked and serve with freshly cooked rice and some chopped coriander.

TUNA RISOTTO

A good risotto usually needs a lot of attention to make sure that it doesn't dry out while allowing the rice to absorb all the liquid. Using a slow cooker means you can leave it and it will still be moist.

INGREDIENTS *Serves 4*

30g/1oz butter
2 spring onions, finely chopped
1 small courgette, diced
225g/8oz quick-cook white rice
750ml/1¼ pints fish stock (see p.22)
120ml/4fl oz dry white wine
450g/1lb tuna, skinned and diced
salt and freshly ground black pepper
3 tbsp chopped fresh tarragon

METHOD

1. Put the butter in the crock and turn the setting to HIGH. Once the butter has melted, add the spring onions and courgette and stir until they are coated in the butter. Cover and cook for 30 minutes.

2. Parboil the rice for 5 minutes, drain and add to the crock. Pour in the stock and wine, cover and cook for 45 minutes, stirring once halfway through cooking time.

3. Add the diced tuna and season to taste with salt and pepper. Cover and cook for a further 15–20 minutes, or until the tuna is cooked. Turn the slow cooker off and leave the risotto to stand for a further 5 minutes.

4. Stir in the fresh tarragon and serve immediately, spooning onto warmed plates.

VARIATIONS

Salmon and prawns work equally well and you can vary the vegetables by adding peas or cucumber instead of courgette.

PART 5

MEAT

Many people choose to buy a slow cooker because it means they can use cheaper cuts of meat, which are best when cooked for a long time at a low heat. The slow cooker helps to tenderize the meat and makes it tastier and much easier to eat. Examples are chuck steak, lamb shanks, pork shoulder and skirt steak.

COOKING MEAT

Whatever type of meat you choose, you'll find that the slow-cooker method results in tender, moist flesh.

Beef can be turned into a succulent, tender meal with ease in the slow cooker. Cuts from the neck, shoulder and lower leg need a longer cooking time and are therefore not suitable for roasting; they can, however, be used to make mouth-watering stews, casseroles or pot roasts without the need for marinating first to help break down the tough sinews. The taste can be enhanced with strong flavours such as horseradish or the more subtle flavours of vegetables and herbs. Any excess fat should be cut off the meat first, as this would break down and spoil the flavour of the gravy.

Lamb has a natural sweet taste that improves with slow cooking. It is used all round the world in dishes such as tagines, where fruit is often added to enhance the flavour. Herbs such as mint are also a common accompaniment.

The most popular cuts of lamb for slow cooking come from the legs and neck, both of which are relatively cheap; lamb shank is usually cooked on the bone, which allows the meat to absorb flavour from the bone marrow. Lamb is also popular in curries, stews and casseroles, or can be stuffed to make a lovely pot roast.

Pork is also versatile when it comes to slow cooking and virtually all the cuts can be used. Neck end, tenderloin, shoulder and fillets all work well and many of the processed products from pork such as bacon and sausages can be turned into tasty meals. Pork goes very well with any vegetable or, for something a little different, try fruit such as apples, apricots or cranberries.

BEEF BOURGUIGNON

This rich beef dish makes a great winter supper and the slow cooker version makes the meat melt in your mouth.

INGREDIENTS *Serves 4*

4 rashers of streaky bacon, cut into strips
450g/1lb braising steak, diced
2 tbsp plain flour
2 tsp olive oil
1 carrot, sliced
1 onion, chopped
2 garlic cloves, minced
375ml/13fl oz red wine
375ml/13fl oz brown meat stock (see p.20)
1 tbsp tomato purée
1 tsp dried thyme
2 bay leaves
12 small shallots, peeled
175g/6oz button mushrooms

METHOD

1. Turn your slow cooker to HIGH.

2. Put the bacon and 1 tablespoon of water in a frying pan and cook for 5 minutes, or until the bacon is starting to go brown and the water has evaporated. Transfer to the crock of the slow cooker.

3. Put the braising steak into the frying pan and sauté until it is browned on all sides. Once it is brown, add 1 tablespoon of flour and stir until the beef is coated. Add the beef to the slow cooker.

4. Using the same pan, heat the olive oil and add the carrot, onion and garlic. Cook for about 5 minutes, or until they start to soften. Add the remaining ingredients and bring to the boil.

5. Pour the contents of the frying pan into the slow cooker, turn the heat down to LOW, cover, and cook for 8 hours. Remove the bay leaves. Mix the remaining flour with a little of the gravy and then add to the slow cooker. Cook, uncovered, for a further 30 minutes or until thickened.

BEEF CURRY

Because a slow cooker allows all the flavours to infuse, curries are perfect when made this way. Serve this one with nutty brown rice.

INGREDIENTS *Serves 4–6*

4 tbsp olive oil
800g/1¾lb braising steak, cubed
2 onions, finely chopped
4 garlic cloves, finely chopped
2 green chillies, deseeded and finely chopped
2.5cm/1in fresh root ginger, peeled and grated
4 tsp ground cumin
4 tsp ground coriander
2 tsp ground turmeric
2 × 400g/14oz cans chopped tomatoes
2 tsp garam masala
200g/7oz natural yogurt
225g/8oz baby spinach leaves

METHOD

1. Turn the slow cooker to HIGH.
2. Heat half of the oil in a frying pan and fry the beef cubes for about 5 minutes, or until they are brown on all sides. Tip the meat into the crock of the slow cooker.
3. Heat the remaining oil and fry the onions for 5 minutes, then add the garlic, chilli and ginger and fry for another 2 minutes. Add all the spices except the garam masala and fry for a further minute. Tip the contents of the frying pan into the crock.
4. Add the tomatoes to the crock and then fill one of the empty cans with water and pour it into the crock. Stir everything thoroughly and press down the meat so that it is completely immersed in liquid. Turn the heat down to LOW, cover, and cook for 8–10 hours.
5. During the last 20 minutes of cooking, add the garam masala, yogurt and spinach, stir to combine and leave to finish cooking. The curry can be kept warm until you are ready to serve.

BOLOGNESE SAUCE

This is a slow-cooker version of the traditional Bolognese sauce, but with the addition of Italian sausage for extra depth of flavour.

INGREDIENTS *Serves 8*

225g/8oz Italian sausage
2 tsp olive oil
450g/1lb minced beef
1 small onion, finely chopped
1 small carrot, grated
2 celery sticks, finely chopped
2 garlic cloves, crushed
2 × 400g/14oz cans chopped tomatoes
115g/4oz tomato purée
1 tsp sugar
2 tsp dried oregano
2 tsp dried basil
120ml/4fl oz red wine
salt and freshly ground black pepper
pasta and grated Parmesan cheese, to serve

METHOD

1. Turn the slow cooker to HIGH.

2. Remove the skin from the Italian sausage and break into small pieces. Heat the oil in a frying pan and brown the minced beef and sausage, stirring to stop it from sticking.

3. Once the meat is browned, add the onion, carrot, celery and garlic and cook for about 5 minutes, or until the onion is tender. Drain well.

4. Transfer the mixture into the crock of your slow cooker. Add the remaining ingredients except the pasta and cheese, cover with a lid and cook on LOW for 6 hours.

5. Serve over your favourite type of pasta, sprinkled liberally with Parmesan cheese.

BRAISED BEEF & MUSHROOM

This is great comfort food, with its rich gravy and tender meat – perfect served over creamy mashed potatoes.

INGREDIENTS *Serves 6*

1.8kg/4lb chuck steak, trimmed of fat
2 strips of pared zest from 1 orange
1 onion, finely chopped
250ml/8fl oz brown meat stock (see p.20)
60ml/2fl oz dry sherry
2 tbsp balsamic vinegar
2 tbsp soy sauce
1 tsp dried thyme
2.5cm/1in fresh root ginger, peeled and grated
salt and freshly ground black pepper
450g/1lb wide cap mushrooms, sliced
2 tbsp oil
2 tbsp cornflour

METHOD

1. Cut the beef into 2.5cm/1in cubes. Place them in the crock.

2. In a large saucepan, combine the orange zest, onion, stock, sherry, vinegar, soy sauce, thyme and ginger. Season to taste. Bring to the boil and then pour over the meat in the crock. Cover with the lid, turn the heat to HIGH and cook for 5–6 hours, or until the meat is very tender.

3. Cut the mushrooms in half lengthwise and fry in the oil until soft and lightly browned.

4. Lift the meat from the slow cooker and keep warm. Skim any fat off the surface of the liquid in the crock, then put the liquid into a pan and boil over a high heat until it has reduced by one-third. Mix the cornflour with a little water and add to the gravy, stirring until it has thickened.

5. Spoon the mushrooms on top of the meat and pour the thickened gravy over.

BRAISED OXTAIL & ONION

Oxtail is often overlooked these days as it requires long, slow cooking, but it can be left to its own devices in the slow cooker.

INGREDIENTS *Serves 4*

1 tbsp olive oil
900g/2lb oxtail, trimmed
2 large onions, finely chopped
2 tbsp plain flour
250ml/8fl oz ruby port
450ml/15fl oz brown meat stock (see p.20)
1 cinnamon stick, halved
1 tsp ground mace
2 tsp juniper berries, crushed
2 tsp tomato purée
salt and freshly ground black pepper
1 red pepper, cut in half
400g/14oz can cannellini beans
1 tbsp freshly chopped basil

METHOD

1. Turn the slow cooker to HIGH.
2. Heat the oil in a frying pan and add the oxtail. Cook to seal, turning, so that it is browned on all sides. Lift out and place in the crock of the slow cooker.
3. Add the onions to the pan and fry for 5 minutes until golden brown. Mix in the flour, then gradually add the port and stock and stir to combine. Add the cinnamon, mace, juniper berries and tomato purée and season to taste. Bring to the boil, stirring.
4. Pour the stock mixture over the oxtail in the slow cooker, turn the heat down to LOW, cover and cook for 9–10 hours.
5. Just before serving, grill the red pepper under a hot grill for a few minutes, turning until the skin is charred. Allow to cool and then peel off the skin and cut the flesh into slices.
6. Mix the beans and fresh basil together and heat through in a saucepan. Serve the oxtail over the top of the beans and garnish with the red pepper slices.

BRISKET OF BEEF

Brisket of beef makes a wonderful, succulent pot roast and with just a few vegetables and some beef stock you have a meal to be proud of with very little effort.

INGREDIENTS *Serves 6*

1.1kg/2½lb rolled brisket of beef
salt and freshly ground black pepper
30g/1oz beef dripping
2 onions, cut into quarters
2 carrots, cut into quarters
2 celery sticks, sliced
2 bay leaves
2 sprigs of fresh thyme
300ml/10fl oz hot brown meat stock (see p.20)

METHOD

1. Season the meat with salt and pepper, then heat the dripping in a large frying pan. Seal the meat by cooking on a high heat until it is browned on all sides.

2. Lift out the meat and set aside. Drain off half the fat in the pan and then add the vegetables. Cook until they are slightly tender and have started to go brown.

3. Arrange some of the vegetables in the crock, put the brisket on top and lay the remaining vegetables around the sides. Add the bay leaves and thyme and then pour in the hot meat stock.

4. Cover with the lid and cook on HIGH for 4 hours. Reduce the heat to LOW and cook for a further 2–3 hours, basting the meat with the juices once or twice to make sure it stays moist.

5. When the meat is tender, remove it from the crock and leave to stand, covered in foil, for 15 minutes before carving.

6. Skim off any excess fat from the juices in the crock, then put the liquid and vegetables into a food processor and blend until smooth for a rich gravy.

CHILLI CON CARNE

This recipe has been adapted for the slow cooker. The flavour is just as good, if not better, than in a chilli con carne cooked on the hob.

INGREDIENTS *Serves 4*

2 tbsp olive oil
4 large shallots, finely chopped
2 garlic cloves, finely chopped
1 green pepper, deseeded and chopped
450g/1lb minced beef
2 tsp hot chilli powder
1 tbsp plain flour
1 tsp brown sugar
4 tbsp tomato purée
400g/14oz can chopped tomatoes
2 fresh tomatoes, skinned and chopped
1 bay leaf
1 tsp dried thyme
salt and freshly ground black pepper
400g/14oz can kidney beans, drained

METHOD

1. Heat the oil in a frying pan and add the shallots, garlic and green pepper. Fry, stirring, for 5 minutes until they are soft and lightly browned.

2. Add the minced beef and fry until lightly browned.

3. Blend together the chilli powder, flour, brown sugar and tomato purée to form a paste. Stir the paste into the pan, together with the canned and fresh tomatoes. Add the bay leaf and dried thyme and season to taste.

4. Tip all the contents of the frying pan into the slow cooker, cover, and cook for 3 hours on HIGH or 6 hours on LOW, depending on how much time you have.

5. One hour before serving, add the kidney beans and stir to combine.

6. Serve with rice or spooned over jacket potatoes, or even on top of warmed nachos and cheese.

LAMB HOTPOT

This is a famous dish of lamb and potatoes that originated in Lancashire. It is one that can easily be adapted for the slow cooker.

INGREDIENTS *Serves 4*

750g/1lb 10oz lean boneless lamb, cubed
60g/2oz plain flour, seasoned with salt and black pepper
1 tbsp olive oil
2 onions, sliced
1 garlic clove, finely chopped
2 celery sticks, sliced
1 carrot, sliced
115g/4oz swede, cubed
salt and freshly ground black pepper
½ tsp mustard powder
½ tsp freshly grated nutmeg
3 bay leaves
1 tsp dried rosemary
1 tsp dried thyme
450g/1lb potatoes, peeled and sliced
2 tbsp dry sherry
400ml/14fl oz meat stock (see p.20)

METHOD

1. Toss the lamb in the seasoned flour. Heat the oil in a large frying pan and add the lamb. Cook until it is nicely browned on all sides.

2. Layer the meat in the crock of your slow cooker with the onions, garlic, celery, carrot and swede and season to taste with salt and pepper.

3. Add the mustard, nutmeg, bay leaves, rosemary and thyme and then cover with the potato slices. Pour in the sherry and stock, cover, and cook on HIGH for 4 hours.

LAMB WITH APRICOTS

The lamb stays wonderfully tender in this recipe and the addition of apricots gives it a sharp and tangy flavour.

INGREDIENTS *Serves 4*

550g/1¼lb braising lamb
2 tbsp plain flour, seasoned with salt and black pepper
2 tbsp olive oil
1 onion, finely chopped
2 garlic cloves, crushed
600ml/1 pint chicken stock (see p.21)
grated zest and juice of 1 orange
1 cinnamon stick
1 tsp clear honey
175g/6oz dried apricots
3 tbsp fresh mint, chopped
30g/1oz ground almonds
30g/1oz flaked almonds, toasted

METHOD

1. Trim all the fat and gristle from the lamb and cut into 2.5cm/1in cubes. Toss the lamb in the seasoned flour until it is completely coated.

2. Heat the oil in a large frying pan, add the lamb and cook for 3–4 minutes or until it is evenly browned. Remove the lamb with a slotted spoon and place in the crock of your slow cooker.

3. Add the onion and garlic to the frying pan and cook gently for 5 minutes, or until softened. Add this to the crock along with the remaining ingredients, with the exception of the ground and flaked almonds.

4. Turn the cooker setting to HIGH, cover and cook for 1 hour. Turn the heat down to LOW and continue cooking for a further 6–8 hours or until the lamb is really tender. Just before the end of the cooking time, stir in the ground almonds.

5. Serve over couscous topped with the toasted flaked almonds. Add some chopped apricots as well if you like extra fruit.

LIVER & BACON CASSEROLE

Liver produces a lovely rich gravy and this dish is complemented by creamy mustard mashed potatoes to soak it up.

INGREDIENTS *Serves 4*

675g/1½lb lamb's liver, cut into 3mm/⅛in slivers
60g/2oz plain flour, seasoned with salt and black pepper
1 tbsp olive oil
4 rashers of smoked bacon, cut into 2.5cm/1in slices
2 onions, thinly sliced
2 large cooking apples, peeled, cored and thinly sliced
400g/14oz can chopped tomatoes
200ml/7fl oz brown meat stock (see p.20)
salt and freshly ground black pepper

METHOD

1. Toss the lamb's liver in the seasoned flour. Heat the oil in a large frying pan and cook the liver for 3 minutes until it is browned on both sides. Remove from the pan and set aside.

2. Add the bacon and onions to the same pan and fry until they are browned.

3. Put half the apple slices and half the bacon and onion mixture into the crock of your slow cooker, add the liver and then lay the remaining apple slices and bacon and onion mixture over the top. Mix the tomatoes and stock and pour into the crock. Check for seasoning, cover and cook on HIGH for 3–4 hours under tender.

MUSTARD MASH

For the mustard mash, boil 4 medium potatoes and then mash them with 2 tbsp single cream and 1 tbsp wholegrain mustard.

MARMALADE-GLAZED GAMMON

The slow cooker is by far the easiest way to cook your Christmas ham, giving you much more time to wrap your presents!

INGREDIENTS *Serves 12*

1.35kg/3lb middle cut gammon joint, soaked overnight
30 whole cloves
750ml/1¼pt cloudy apple juice
200g/7oz soft dark brown sugar
2 tsp ground cinnamon
1 tsp freshly grated nutmeg
2 tsp ground ginger
1 tsp ground cloves
grated zest of 1 orange
115g/4oz fine cut orange marmalade

METHOD

1. Using a sharp knife, score the fat on the gammon joint into a neat diamond pattern. Press a single clove into the centre of each diamond. Place the gammon in the slow cooker and pour in the apple juice, leaving about 5cm/2in of the gammon above the surface.

2. Pack the brown sugar on top of the gammon, pressing it into the cuts in the fat. Add the cinnamon, nutmeg, ginger, ground cloves and orange zest, cover and cook on HIGH for 1 hour. Turn the heat down to LOW and cook for a further 8–10 hours.

3. When the gammon is cooked, remove it from the slow cooker and place it in a roasting tin lined with kitchen foil. Heat the marmalade in a saucepan until it becomes liquid and then pour it over the surface of the gammon. Roast in a preheated oven at 200°C/400°F/gas mark 6 for about 20–30 minutes or until the fat is nicely browned and glazed. Baste a couple of times during the roasting time.

4. If you are serving the gammon hot, allow it to rest for 20 minutes before slicing.

MOUSSAKA

This slow-cooked version of the Greek dish made with aubergines is every bit as good as the oven-baked variety.

INGREDIENTS *Serves 4*

2 medium-sized aubergines, thinly sliced lengthways
1 tbsp salt
½ small butternut squash, peeled, deseeded and thinly sliced
4 tbsp olive oil
1 onion, finely chopped
2 garlic cloves, finely chopped
450g/1lb minced lamb
400g/14oz can chopped tomatoes
1 tsp dried oregano
1 tsp ground cinnamon
salt and freshly ground black pepper
50g/1¾oz butter
60g/2oz plain flour
1 tsp mustard powder
600ml/1 pint milk
100g/3½oz Cheddar cheese, grated
½ tsp freshly grated nutmeg
1 egg yolk
2 tbsp fresh white breadcrumbs

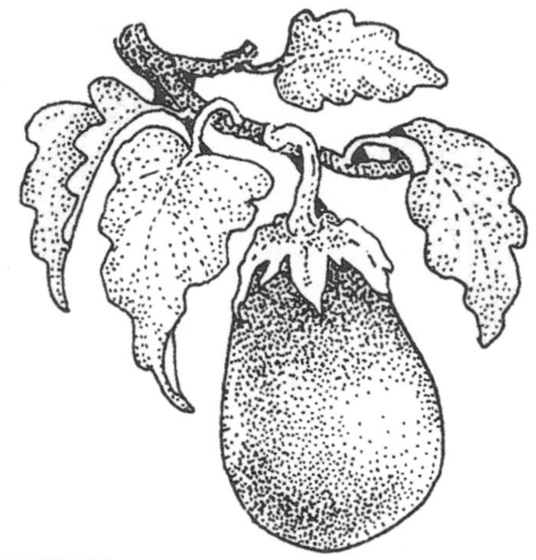

METHOD

1. Lay the aubergine slices in a large colander and sprinkle with the salt. Leave for 30 minutes to allow the liquid to drain from the aubergines and then rinse them under cold water to remove the salt. Pat dry with kitchen towel.

2. Brush the aubergine and butternut squash slices with half the olive oil and then put them in a single layer on a baking tray.

Place under a hot grill and cook for 5 minutes each side until they are soft and lightly browned.

3. Place half the aubergine and butternut squash slices in the crock of the slow cooker and turn the cooker to HIGH.

4. Heat the remaining olive oil in a large frying pan and cook the onion until softened and translucent. Add the garlic and the minced lamb and cook until the meat is browned.

5. Add the tomatoes, oregano and cinnamon and season to taste with salt and pepper. Allow the mixture to come to the boil, then pour it over the contents in the slow cooker. Place the remaining aubergine and butternut squash slices on top, cover, and cook on HIGH for 2 hours.

6. Towards the end of the 2 hours, prepare the cheese topping. Melt the butter in a saucepan, add the flour and mustard powder and stir over a medium heat until the flour has cooked and the mixture starts to come away from the sides of the pan. Warm the milk and gradually add this to the pan, stirring constantly. Cook over a medium–high heat, stirring, until the sauce has thickened. Remove the pan from the heat and stir in two-thirds of the grated cheese and the nutmeg. Allow to cool, then beat in the egg yolk.

7. Pour the sauce into the crock, cover, and cook for an additional 2 hours.

8. Just before serving, remove the lid from the crock and sprinkle over the breadcrumbs and remaining cheese. Take out the crock and put it under a hot grill for several minutes to brown.

VARIATIONS

If you want to add even more vegetables, use some slices of courgette and thin slices of potato and cook them with the other vegetables.

PORK STUFFED WITH APRICOTS

Almost any fruit goes well with pork, and this combination of pork and apricots provides lovely flavours.

INGREDIENTS *Serves 4*

1 tbsp butter
2 banana shallots, finely chopped
175g/6oz butternut squash, peeled, deseeded and diced
1 tsp finely grated orange zest
115g/4oz dried apricots, chopped
30g/1oz fresh white breadcrumbs
1 tbsp chopped fresh parsley
1 tbsp chopped fresh chives
salt and freshly ground black pepper
2 × 225g/8oz pork fillets
6 slices Parma ham
1 tbsp olive oil
150ml/5fl oz dry white wine

METHOD

1. To make the stuffing, melt the butter in a frying pan and add the shallots and squash. Fry until they are soft. Tip them into a bowl and mash down with a fork. Add the orange zest, apricots, breadcrumbs, parsley and chives and season with salt and pepper.

2. Slice down the length of both pork fillets, three-quarters of the way through. Fill both cavities with the stuffing.

3. Lay 3 slices of Parma ham on a work surface so that they slightly overlap. Lay a pork fillet in the centre and fold the ham round to completely seal the pork. Repeat with the remaining ham and pork fillet. Secure with wooden cocktail sticks.

4. Heat the olive oil in a clean pan and fry the pork parcels on both sides to brown. Transfer to the slow cooker, pour in the wine, cover, and cook on HIGH for 1 hour. Turn the heat to LOW and cook for a further 2–3 hours, or until the pork is tender.

POT-ROAST SHOULDER OF LAMB

Shoulder is one of the cheaper cuts of lamb, but if pot-roasted it is moist and tender – and a great alternative to a normal roast.

INGREDIENTS *Serves 6*

1 tbsp olive oil
1.35kg/3lb shoulder of lamb, trimmed, boned and rolled
2 garlic cloves, quartered
8 fresh sprigs of rosemary
1 onion, finely chopped
2 carrots, finely chopped
3 celery sticks, finely chopped
1 leek, finely chopped
150ml/5fl oz red wine
300ml/10fl oz chicken or vegetable stock (see pp.21 and 23)
400g/14oz can chopped tomatoes
1 tsp dried thyme
2 bay leaves
400g/14oz can butter beans

METHOD

1. Heat the oil in a large frying pan and cook the lamb until it is brown on all sides. Remove from the pan and set aside.

2. When the lamb is cool enough to handle, make some deep cuts in the meat with the point of a knife and push a piece of garlic and a small sprig of rosemary into each one.

3. In the same pan, fry the onion, carrot, celery and leek until they are soft and then transfer them to the crock of your slow cooker. Lay the lamb on top of the vegetables and then add the wine, stock, tomatoes, thyme and bay leaves. Cover and cook on HIGH for 4 hours.

4. Lift the lamb out of the pot, add the butter beans and stir them into the vegetable mixture. Return the lamb to the crock and cook for a further 2 hours on HIGH or until the lamb is tender.

5. Leave the lamb to rest for 10 minutes before slicing.

SAUSAGE & SAGE CASSEROLE

This is a tasty casserole that takes very little preparation and one that will be popular with the children.

INGREDIENTS *Serves 4*

1 tsp olive oil
8 pork sausages, cut into bite-sized pieces
1 onion, sliced
2 carrots, chopped
1 leek, finely sliced
2 garlic cloves, finely chopped
1 tbsp plain flour
300ml/10fl oz hot vegetable stock (see p.23)
1 tbsp tomato purée
60g/2oz fresh sage, finely chopped
salt and freshly ground black pepper

METHOD

1. Heat the oil in a frying pan and add the sausage pieces. Keep turning until they are just browned on all sides and then put them into the crock of your slow cooker.

2. Drain off most of the fat from the pan and then add the onion and fry for about 5 minutes or until it is softened and browned.

3. Add the carrots, leek and garlic and fry for another 2 minutes to soften. Sprinkle the flour over the vegetable mixture and then add the hot stock. Stir to combine all the flour from the bottom of the pan. Add the tomato purée and fresh sage and then add to the slow cooker.

4. Cover and cook on HIGH for 1 hour, then turn down to LOW and cook for a further 6 hours. Serve with some baby new potatoes and garden peas.

SOMERSET PORK

Cider and tender pork are a perfect combination, and left to cook all day they make a wonderful supper dish.

INGREDIENTS *Serves 4*

30g/1oz butter
4 boneless loin chops
1 large onion, sliced
1 garlic clove, finely sliced
2 sweet eating apples, peeled, cored and cut into rings
1 tsp sugar
1 tsp dried thyme
salt and freshly ground black pepper
250ml/8fl oz dry cider
3 tbsp double cream

METHOD

1. Heat the slow cooker to HIGH.
2. Melt the butter in a large frying pan and fry the pork chops on both sides until they are golden brown. Remove the chops and place them in the crock of the slow cooker.
3. Add the onion and garlic to the same pan and fry for 5 minutes until softened and lightly browned. Put the onions and garlic into the crock.
4. Add a little more butter if necessary and then fry the apple rings for a few seconds on each side just to give them a little colour. Transfer them to the slow cooker and sprinkle with the sugar. Add the thyme and season with a little salt and pepper.
5. Pour in the cider, cover the pan and cook on HIGH for 1 hour. Turn the heat down to LOW and cook for a further 4–5 hours or until the meat is really tender.
6. Remove the chops from the slow cooker and place on warmed plates. Stir the cream into the sauce and then pour over the chops. Serve with your favourite vegetables and sauté potatoes.

SPICY PORK RIBS

If you like pork ribs, try this Chinese-style recipe where the meat is coated in a lovely sticky, hot sauce and just falls off the bone.

INGREDIENTS *Serves 4*

675g/1½lb pork ribs
3 tbsp cornflour, seasoned with salt and black pepper
75ml/2½fl oz soy sauce
1 tbsp peach jam
120ml/4fl oz water
1 large tomato, skinned and diced
2 garlic cloves, crushed
1 Scotch bonnet chilli, finely chopped

METHOD

1. Toss the pork ribs in the seasoned cornflour and lay them in the crock of the slow cooker. Add all the other ingredients, cover, and cook on LOW for 6–8 hours, or until the ribs are very tender. Turn the ribs halfway through the cooking time to make sure they are evenly cooked.

2. Remove the lid from the cooker and turn the heat up to HIGH. Cook for a further 1–2 hours, uncovered, or until the sauce has reduced by about half.

NOODLE STIR-FRY

1 tbsp sesame oil
1 green pepper, 1 yellow pepper, sliced
115g/4oz French beans, sliced
1 packet chow mein noodles
1 tbsp rice wine vinegar
juice of 1 lemon

Heat the oil in a wok, add the peppers and green beans and cook for 4–5 minutes, stirring. Add the noodles, vinegar and lemon juice and toss to combine.

STEAK & KIDNEY PIE

This pie has a rich and glossy gravy due to the addition of stout.

INGREDIENTS *Serves 4*
675g/1½lb stewing steak
225g/8oz lamb's kidneys
3 tbsp olive oil
2 onions, finely chopped
2 tbsp plain flour
200ml/7fl oz meat stock (see p.20)
100ml/3½fl oz stout
1 tbsp tomato purée
2 bay leaves
salt and freshly ground
black pepper
350g/12oz puff pastry
1 beaten egg, to glaze
1 tbsp chopped fresh parsley

METHOD

1. Trim the meat of any fat, and then cut into 2.5cm/1in cubes. Remove the skin and core from the kidneys and cut into slices.

2. Heat half the oil in a frying pan and add the steak. Sauté until it is brown on all sides. Transfer to the crock using a slotted spoon. Turn the slow cooker to HIGH.

3. Add the kidneys to the frying pan and brown, then transfer them to the crock.

4. Add the remaining oil and then fry the onion until it is soft and just starting to turn brown. Sprinkle the flour over the onions and stir to combine. Gradually stir in the stock, stout and tomato purée and bring to the boil, stirring, until the gravy thickens. Add this to the crock and cover. Reduce the setting to LOW and cook for 5–7 hours.

5. Towards the end of the cooking time, roll out the pastry and cut a large circle. Glaze with egg and place on a baking tray. Bake in a preheated oven at 200°C/400°F/ gas mark 6 for 25 minutes.

6. Stir the fresh parsley into the meat, and spoon onto warmed serving plates with a slice of the pastry crust on top.

VEAL STEW

The light and delicate flavour of the veal combined with vegetables makes this a great dish to eat with warm, crusty bread.

INGREDIENTS *Serves 4*

2 tbsp plain flour
½ tsp salt
½ tsp freshly grated nutmeg
½ tsp white pepper
675g/1½lb boneless veal shoulder, trimmed and cut into cubes
2 tbsp vegetable oil
4 potatoes, peeled and cubed
1 small onion, finely chopped
225g/8oz button mushrooms, quartered
300ml/10fl oz chicken stock (see p.21)
200ml/7fl oz sour cream
chopped fresh parsley, to garnish

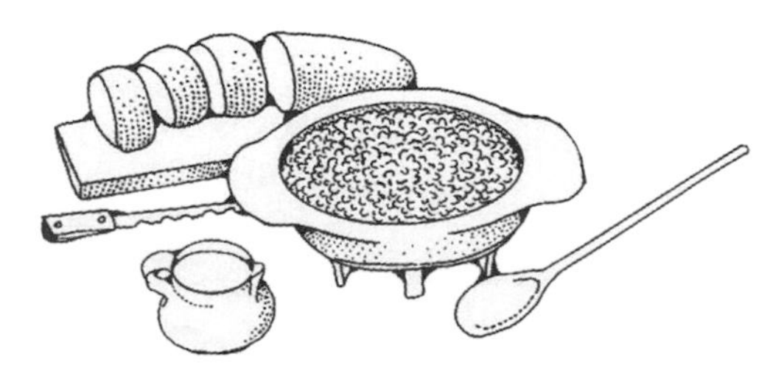

METHOD

1. Mix the flour, salt, nutmeg and pepper in a large freezer bag. Put a few pieces of the veal inside the bag, seal and shake to coat them in the flour. Repeat with the remaining veal.

2. Heat the oil in a frying pan and fry the veal until it is well browned on all sides. Transfer the meat to the slow cooker and turn it to HIGH.

3. Add the potatoes, onion, mushrooms and stock to the crock and stir to combine. Cover and cook for 1 hour. Reduce the heat to LOW and cook for 6–7 hours or until the meat and vegetables are tender.

4. Just before you are ready to serve, stir in the sour cream. Spoon the stew onto warmed serving plates and garnish with chopped parsley.

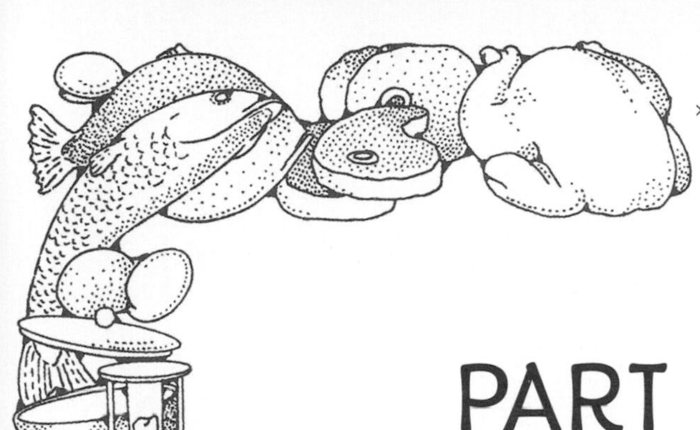

PART 6

POULTRY & GAME

'Poultry' covers a wide range of birds including chicken, turkey, goose, duck and guinea fowl, while 'game' includes rabbits and venison as well as birds such as pheasant, quail and partridge. Any of these can be cooked in the slow cooker, though larger birds such as turkey will need to be cut into portions first.

COOKING POULTRY & GAME

Although chicken is by far the most popular choice for most people, it is good idea to be a little more adventurous as you become accustomed to cooking in your slow cooker.

Poultry is often the choice for busy mums and dads as it is widely available, inexpensive, very lean and healthy, and most of all extremely versatile as it will go with most vegetable flavours. The smaller birds can be cooked whole as a pot-roast, helping them to retain their natural succulence, or cut into joints if they are too large to fit. As a general rule, a 900g/2lb bird will feed a family of four.

If you use frozen poultry it is very important to make sure that it is thoroughly thawed before being cooked. Ideally it should be left to thaw in the refrigerator, so you will need to plan in advance as this can take as long as 30 hours. Remember, once you have thawed poultry it cannot be refrozen unless it is cooked first.

When you are cooking a whole bird, don't forget to keep the carcass for making stock (see p.21).

Because of their high fat content, ducks and geese are not suitable for cooking whole in a slow cooker but you can use smaller joints, such as the breast, which are leaner. Venison, rabbit and wild boar are all suitable for cooking in the slow cooker. Rabbit is probably one of the best choices when you are starting to cook game as it comes in compact joints and doesn't require a lot of complicated preparation.

The majority of game benefits from being hung before being cooked, but if you buy it from a reliable butcher this will already have been done for you.

CARIBBEAN CHICKEN

The spicy sauce in this recipe penetrates the meat and helps to make it really tender and moist.

INGREDIENTS *Serves 4*

1 tbsp vegetable oil
1 tbsp unsalted butter
8 skinless chicken pieces, such as thighs and legs

FOR THE SAUCE:

4 spring onions, chopped
2 garlic cloves, crushed
1 hot red chilli pepper, deseeded and finely chopped
1 tsp ground allspice
1 tsp ground cinnamon
1 tsp dried thyme
¼ tsp freshly grated nutmeg
2 tsp dark brown sugar
1 tbsp plain flour
300ml/10fl oz chicken stock (see p.21)
1 tbsp lime juice
1 tbsp white wine vinegar
2 tsp tomato purée
salt and freshly ground black pepper

METHOD

1. Heat the oil and butter in a large frying pan and cook the chicken pieces in batches until they are brown on all sides. Lift the chicken out with a slotted spoon and transfer to the crock of your slow cooker.

2. Add the spring onions, garlic and chilli to the frying pan and cook for 5 minutes or until the onion is soft. Stir in the spices, sugar and flour until they are all combined. Slowly add the chicken stock, stirring until it has thickened. Remove from the heat.

3. Stir in the lime juice, vinegar and tomato purée and season to taste. Pour the sauce over the chicken in the slow cooker, cover with a lid and cook on HIGH for 3–4 hours, or until the chicken is cooked. Serve with brown rice and some chopped coriander.

CHICKEN FRICASSÉE

With its creamy sauce, this chicken recipe will be an all-time family favourite. You can spice it up with a bit of sherry when making it for a dinner party.

INGREDIENTS *Serves 4*

30g/1oz butter
2 tbsp sunflower oil
1.35kg/3lb boneless chicken breast, cut into pieces
3 tbsp plain flour
250ml/8fl oz dry white wine
600ml/1 pint hot chicken stock (see p.21)
1 *bouquet garni*
1 tsp lemon juice
1 tsp mild smoked paprika
salt and freshly ground black pepper
1 large onion, finely chopped
225g/8oz button mushrooms, left whole
75ml/2½fl oz double cream
2 tbsp chopped fresh parsley

METHOD

1. Melt half the butter and half the oil in a frying pan and add the chicken pieces. Fry until lightly browned on one side, then turn the chicken and repeat on the other side. Remove the chicken with a slotted spoon and place it in the crock of the slow cooker.

3. Stir the flour into the juices left in the frying pan and then gradually blend in the wine and chicken stock. Add the *bouquet* *garni*, lemon juice and paprika and bring to the boil. Season well and pour over the chicken in the crock. Cover with the lid and turn the cooker to HIGH.

4. Clean the frying pan and heat the remaining butter and oil. Add the onion and fry until softened but not brown.

5. Add the button mushrooms to the pan and fry until they are lightly browned. Tip the onions and mushrooms into the slow cooker.

6. Replace the lid on the slow cooker and continue to cook on HIGH for a further 3–4 hours, or until the chicken is cooked through and tender.

7. Carefully lift out the chicken pieces with a slotted spoon and place them on a warmed serving dish together with the vegetables. Keep warm.

8. Remove the bouquet garni and add the cream to the liquid left in the slow cooker. Season to taste with salt and freshly ground black pepper, then add half the parsley to the sauce and whisk so that they are thoroughly combined.

9. Pour the sauce over the top of the chicken and garnish with the remaining parsley. Serve the fricassée over boiled rice or mashed potatoes.

HOW TO CHECK IF A CHICKEN IS COOKED

- Pierce the thickest part of the portion with a skewer – the juices should run clear, not pink.
- For whole chickens, a meat thermometer inserted into the thickest part of the thigh should register 82–85°C/180–185°F.
- For boneless chicken breasts, insert a knife into the meat – they are done when the centres are no longer pink.

CHICKEN WITH CASHEW NUTS

A very quick and easy-to-prepare recipe, this is ideal if you are just starting to use your slow cooker.

INGREDIENTS *Serves 4*

2 tbsp olive oil
2 onions, finely chopped
2 garlic cloves, finely chopped
4 skinless chicken breasts
1 tbsp plain flour
1 tbsp medium curry powder
1 tsp chilli powder
600ml/1 pint hot chicken stock (see p.21)
150ml/5fl oz Greek yogurt
1 tbsp cornflour
115g/4oz unsalted cashew nuts

METHOD

1. Turn the slow cooker to HIGH.

2. Heat the oil in a frying pan and add the onions. Fry for 5 minutes until they are soft but not coloured. Add the garlic and cook for 2 more minutes. Transfer the onions and garlic to the slow cooker using a slotted spoon.

3. In the same pan, fry the chicken pieces until they are brown on both sides. Transfer the chicken to the slow cooker using a slotted spoon.

4. Add the flour, curry powder and chilli powder to the juices left in the pan and stir to combine. Cook for 1 minute before slowly adding the hot chicken stock. Bring to the boil and then pour over the contents of the slow cooker.

5. Cover with the lid, turn the heat down to LOW and cook for 6–8 hours.

6. About 45 minutes from the end of the cooking time, combine the yogurt with the cornflour and add to the slow cooker a little at a time, stirring continuously so that the sauce thickens and does not go lumpy. Add the cashew nuts and replace the lid until the cooking time is up.

CHICKEN CURRY

This is a mild curry with a rich, creamy sauce for those people who do not like their food too hot. If you find it too mild but like the flavour, simply add more chillies when making the paste.

INGREDIENTS *Serves 4*

2 small onions, chopped
3 garlic cloves
4cm/1½in fresh root ginger, peeled
1 medium green chilli, deseeded
1 tbsp sesame oil
4 skinless chicken breasts, cut into chunks
30g/1oz butter
1 tsp cumin seeds, crushed
1 tsp fennel seeds, crushed
4 cardamom pods, crushed
1 tsp hot paprika
1 tsp ground turmeric
¼ tsp ground cinnamon
300ml/10fl oz chicken stock (see p.21)
1 tbsp sugar
1 tsp salt
2 tbsp desiccated coconut
75ml/2½fl oz double cream
2 tbsp ground almonds

METHOD

1. Put the onions, garlic, ginger and chilli into a blender and process until you have a fine paste.

2. Heat the oil in a frying pan and add the chicken pieces. Cook over a high heat, stirring, until they are evenly browned. Add the butter to the pan and, once melted, add the paste. Cook over a medium heat for 3 minutes. Add all the spices and then cook for a further minute.

3. Mix in the chicken stock, sugar, salt and coconut and bring to the boil. Once boiling, transfer to the slow cooker. Cover and cook on LOW for 6–7 hours.

4. Before serving, add the cream and ground nuts and stir to combine. Serve with rice and freshly made naan bread.

CHICKEN IN WHITE WINE

This recipe has been adapted from the traditional French *coq au vin*, and gives you a tender and juicy chicken.

INGREDIENTS *Serves 4*

75g/2½oz plain flour, seasoned with salt and black pepper
8 chicken pieces (legs, thighs or breasts)
3 tbsp extra virgin olive oil
3 rashers of smoked bacon, chopped
1 onion, thinly sliced
450g/1lb red-skinned potatoes, cut into 1cm/½in cubes
225g/8oz button mushrooms, quartered
3 garlic cloves, crushed
4 sprigs of fresh parsley, chopped
3 sprigs of fresh thyme, leaves only
1 bay leaf
250ml/8fl oz chicken stock (see p.21)
250ml/8fl oz white wine

METHOD

1. Put the seasoned flour inside a large freezer bag and add 2 pieces of chicken. Seal the bag and shake until the chicken is covered in flour. Repeat with the remaining joints.

2. Heat half the oil in a large frying pan and fry the chicken in batches until it is brown on all sides. Transfer to a slow cooker with a slotted spoon and turn the setting to HIGH.

3. Add the bacon, onion, potatoes, mushrooms and garlic to the frying pan and cook until lightly browned. Transfer to the slow cooker. Add the parsley, thyme and bay leaf and stir to combine.

4. Pour the stock and wine into the frying pan and bring to the boil, stirring to scrape up any brown bits stuck to the bottom. Pour the hot liquid over the chicken, cover, and cook on HIGH for 5 hours. Remove the bay leaf before serving.

DUCK STEW WITH GRAPES

Duck is a rich meat, but adding sweet onions and grapes to the recipe balances the flavours perfectly.

INGREDIENTS *Serves 4*

4 duck breasts
225g/8oz baby shallots, peeled but left whole
½ tsp caster sugar
2 tbsp plain flour
250ml/8fl oz red wine
250ml/8fl oz chicken stock (see p.21)
1 *bouquet garni*
salt and freshly ground black pepper
115g/4oz red seedless grapes, halved

METHOD

1. Heat a frying pan and fry the duck breasts, skin-side down, until golden brown. Turn and cook on the other side. Remove the duck from the pan with a slotted spoon and place in the crock of your slow cooker. Turn the cooker setting to HIGH.

2. Drain off most of the duck fat from the pan and add the shallots. Cook over a medium heat until they start to brown. Sprinkle with the sugar and cook for 5 minutes, stirring frequently. Gradually add the flour and cook for 2 minutes, stirring frequently.

3. Slowly pour the red wine and stock into the frying pan and bring to the boil, stirring. Pour the contents of the pan over the duck. Add the *bouquet garni*, season to taste, cover and cook on HIGH for 1 hour. Turn the cooker to LOW and cook for a further 4–5 hours until the meat is tender.

4. Pour some boiling water over the grapes, then add them to the slow cooker. Cover and cook for a further 30 minutes.

5. Discard the *bouquet garni*, then serve the stew on warmed plates with mashed potato.

GUINEA FOWL WINTER WARMER

Because guinea fowl is a very lean meat it needs to be kept moist during cooking to prevent it from drying out, so slow cooking is ideal.

INGREDIENTS *Serves 6*

4 guinea fowl portions
75g/2½oz plain flour, seasoned with salt and black pepper
3 tbsp olive oil
115g/4oz smoked bacon, chopped
30g/1oz unsalted butter
1 onion, finely chopped
2 garlic cloves, crushed
400ml/14fl oz hot chicken stock (see p.21)
1 tbsp tomato purée
200g/7oz carrots, chopped
2 leeks, sliced
1 sweet potato, chopped
1 tsp fresh thyme leaves
2 bay leaves
2 tsp coarse-grained mustard
200g/7oz button mushrooms

METHOD

1. Coat the guinea fowl portions with seasoned flour.

2. Heat 2 tablespoons of the oil in a frying pan and fry the bacon and guinea fowl until they are browned on all sides. Set aside.

3. Heat the remaining oil and the butter in the frying pan and sauté the onion and garlic until soft but not browned. Add any remaining seasoned flour to the pan and cook for 1 minute, stirring. Stir in the hot stock and tomato purée and cook, stirring, until thickened.

4. Add the carrots, leeks, sweet potato, herbs and mustard to the crock, place the guinea fowl portions on top and pour the liquid from the frying pan over. Cook on HIGH for 1 hour.

5. Turn the guinea fowl portions over and then reduce the heat to LOW and cook for 1 hour. Add the whole mushrooms, stir the contents of the crock and cook for one final hour.

MEDITERRANEAN PHEASANT

Even if you haven't tried cooking pheasant before, this recipe will definitely convert you with its lovely Mediterranean flavours.

INGREDIENTS *Serves 6–8*

75g/2½oz plain flour, seasoned with salt and black pepper
2 pheasants, divided into joints
2 tbsp olive oil
1 onion, sliced
85g/3oz crimini mushrooms, sliced
3 garlic cloves, crushed
250ml/8fl oz dry white wine
250ml/8fl oz chicken stock (see p.21)
85g/3oz black olives, pitted and sliced

METHOD

1. Put the seasoned flour inside a large freezer bag and add 2 pieces of pheasant. Seal the bag and shake until the pheasant is covered in flour. Repeat with the remaining pheasant.

2. Heat the olive oil in a large frying pan over a medium heat. Shake off any excess flour from the pheasant joints and place them in the hot oil. Cook, turning, until the meat is brown on all sides – this should take about 3 minutes each side. Transfer the pheasant to the slow cooker and turn it to HIGH.

3. Cook the onions in the same frying pan until they soften and then stir in the mushrooms and garlic and cook for a further 4–5 minutes.

4. Gradually add the wine and bring to the boil, stirring. Add the stock and bring back to the boil. Pour the liquid over the pheasant in the slow cooker, sprinkle with the sliced olives and cook on HIGH for 4 hours.

4. Serve over crushed new potatoes and a helping of wilted baby spinach.

PEKING DUCK

This is a simple way to prepare that wonderfully flaked duck meat served with plum sauce and extra-thin pancakes.

INGREDIENTS *Serves 4*

FOR THE DUCK:

5 spring onions
1.8–2.25kg/4–5lb whole duck
2.5cm/1in fresh root ginger, peeled
5 whole star anise
2 tsp Chinese 5-spice powder
1 tsp ground cinnamon
½ tsp freshly grated nutmeg
1 tbsp runny honey
2 tbsp soy sauce

FOR THE PLUM SAUCE:

100ml/3½fl oz water
4 red plums, stoned and roughly chopped
2½ tsp caster sugar
1 tbsp runny honey
1 cinnamon stick
1 whole star anise
juice of ½ lime

FOR THE PANCAKES (makes 16):

225g/8oz plain flour
175ml/6fl oz boiling water
2 tbsp sesame oil

FOR THE GARNISH:

6 spring onions, thinly sliced lengthways
½ cucumber, peeled and cut into matchsticks

METHOD FOR THE DUCK

1. First place a small rack or a collapsible steamer in the crock of the slow cooker – because duck contains a lot of fat you need to lift it off the bottom of the crock.

2. Split the spring onions in half lengthways and lay them on top of the rack.

3. Wash and dry the duck and then put the peeled ginger and whole star anise inside the cavity. Score the skin with a sharp knife in several places. Combine the dry spices in a bowl and then rub

them all over the surface of the duck, making sure you get into all the creases.
4. Place the duck, breast-side up, on the rack and pour the honey and soy sauce over. Set the cooker to HIGH and cook for 4–5 hours or until the meat is falling away from the bone.

METHOD FOR THE PLUM SAUCE

Put the water into a small saucepan and bring to the boil. Add the plums, sugar, honey, cinnamon stick and star anise and cook over a medium heat for about 5 minutes, stirring, until the sauce has thickened. Remove from the heat, strain through a fine sieve and then stir in the lime juice.

METHOD FOR THE PANCAKES

1. Sift the flour into a bowl, make a well in the middle and pour in the boiling water. Stir with a wooden spoon until a soft dough is formed. Knead the dough in the bowl for about 5 minutes until it is smooth in texture.
2. Roll the dough into a sausage shape about 30cm/12in long and then divide it into 16 equal pieces. Roll each piece into a small ball. Take two balls, flatten slightly, and then dip one side of one ball in sesame oil. Place the oiled side on top of the other ball and then roll out to form a thin double pancake. The finished pancake should be about 20cm/8in in diameter. Repeat with the remaining dough.
3. Heat the remaining oil in a non-stick frying pan until hot and fry each pancake for about 1 minute on each side, or until lightly coloured. When cool enough, peel the layers apart. Cover with a damp tea towel to prevent them from drying out.

TO SERVE

Pull the duck meat off the bone using two forks and lay it on a warm serving plate. Take a pancake, spread with plum sauce and then fill with duck and sliced onion and cucumber. Roll the pancake up and enjoy.

RABBIT IN TOMATO SAUCE

This is a delicious recipe to serve with spaghetti sprinkled with a liberal helping of Parmesan cheese.

INGREDIENTS *Serves 4*

1 tbsp olive oil
1 small onion, finely chopped
1 small carrot, finely chopped
1 celery stick, finely sliced
½ sweet red pepper, deseeded and finely chopped
1 small red chilli, deseeded and finely chopped
115g/4oz button mushrooms, quartered
2 rashers smoked streaky bacon, chopped
250g/9oz boneless rabbit meat, cut into 1cm/½in pieces
60ml/2fl oz dry white wine
200g/7oz can chopped plum tomatoes
1 tsp dried Italian seasoning
salt and freshly ground black pepper
chopped fresh parsley, to garnish

METHOD

1. Heat the oil in a large frying pan, add the chopped vegetables and bacon and cook for about 5 minutes. Add the rabbit and cook, stirring, until the meat is browned.

2. Transfer the mixture to the slow cooker, turn the setting to HIGH and then add the wine, tomatoes and Italian seasoning. Season to taste with salt and pepper. Stir well, cover and cook on HIGH for 1 hour. Reduce the heat to LOW and then cook for a further 2 hours or until the rabbit is tender.

3. Serve over freshly cooked spaghetti, sprinkled with chopped parsley.

SUMMER RABBIT CASSEROLE

The mild game flavour of the rabbit combined with vegetables makes this a great dish to eat with warm, crusty bread.

INGREDIENTS *Serves 4*

4 rabbit portions
4 tbsp plain flour
1 red onion, finely chopped
1 celery stick, finely sliced
8 baby carrots, topped and tailed
1 sweet red pepper, deseeded and chopped
2 garlic cloves, finely chopped
1 tsp dried thyme
1 tsp Worcestershire sauce
100g/3½oz chorizo, finely chopped
2 × 400g/14oz cans chopped tomatoes
500ml/16fl oz hot vegetable stock (see p.23)
salt and freshly ground white pepper

METHOD

1. Roll the rabbit pieces in the flour and set aside. Keep the surplus flour.

2. Place the onion, celery, carrots and red pepper in the crock of the slow cooker and sprinkle the remaining flour over. Add the garlic, thyme, Worcestershire sauce, chorizo and tomatoes and stir well to combine.

3. Place the rabbit pieces on top of the vegetables and pour the hot stock over. Turn the setting to HIGH, cover and cook for 1 hour. Reduce the heat to LOW and cook for a further 3–4 hours or until the rabbit is falling off the bone.

4. Just before serving, test for seasoning and make sure you add plenty of freshly ground white pepper to give that nice peppery taste.

5. A crisp side salad and a freshly baked crusty loaf are perfect accompaniments to this dish.

TURKEY WITH FRUIT SAUCE

This recipe for turkey is for those people who love the combination of fruit flavours with their meat. Chicken also lends itself extremely well to this fruity sauce.

INGREDIENTS *Serves 4*

1 tbsp olive oil
1.35kg/3lb turkey thighs, skinned and boned
85g/3oz pitted prunes, chopped
85g/3oz dried apricots, chopped
1 eating apple, peeled, cored and diced
1 pear, peeled, cored and diced
120ml/4fl oz orange juice
120ml/4fl oz red wine
4 garlic cloves, minced
2 tbsp runny honey
1 tsp dried thyme
½ tsp dried marjoram
½ tsp salt
¼ tsp white pepper
2 tbsp cornflour
3 tbsp cold water

METHOD

1. Heat the oil in a large frying pan and then add the turkey and cook until it is browned on all sides. Transfer to the crock of the slow cooker with a slotted spoon.

2. Put the fruit into the slow cooker with the turkey.

3. In a bowl, mix together the orange juice, wine, garlic, honey, thyme, marjoram and salt and pepper. Pour this over the turkey and fruit in the slow cooker. Cover and turn the setting to LOW. Cook at this heat for 6–8 hours or until the turkey is tender and cooked all the way through.

4. Before serving, thicken the sauce by mixing the cornflour with the cold water. Pour it into the crock and cook on HIGH for 10–15 minutes, uncovered, or until the sauce has thickened.

5. Serve this dish over couscous or rice and roasted vegetables.

TURKEY WITH WILD RICE STUFFING

The kitchen is always a busy place at Christmas, so why not make your life easier and cook your turkey in the slow cooker.

INGREDIENTS *Serves 8*

350g/12oz wild rice
1 onion, finely chopped
100g/3½oz dried cranberries
2 eating apples, peeled, cored and chopped
1 tsp dried thyme
1 tsp salt
½ tsp freshly ground black pepper
1.35–1.8kg/3–4lb whole turkey crown
750ml/1¼ pints chicken stock (see p.21)

METHOD

1. In a bowl, mix together the wild rice, onion, cranberries, apple, thyme and salt and pepper. Put the mixture into the crock of your slow cooker.

2. Lay the turkey crown on top of the rice mixture and then pour the stock over the top, making sure that all the rice is covered with stock. Cover and cook on LOW for 7–8 hours or until the turkey is thoroughly cooked – if you want to use a meat thermometer, it should read 160°C/325°F when pushed into the thickest part. By this time the rice should be tender.

3. When the turkey is cooked, remove from the crock and leave to rest, covered with foil, for 10–15 minutes before carving. Serve with the stuffing on the side.

CHEF'S TIP

To ensure that the rice doesn't go mushy, always buy a good-quality one with long grains.

WILD BOAR SAUSAGE CASSEROLE

Wild boar has a sweet and nutty flavour that is balanced by the citrus and thyme in this recipe. However, if you can't obtain wild boar sausages, venison sausages will work just as well.

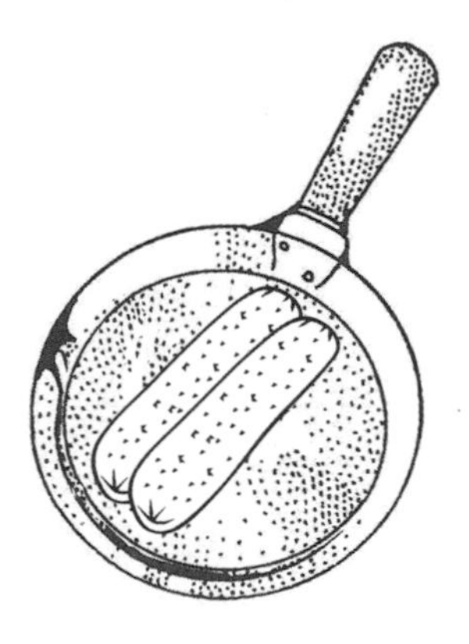

INGREDIENTS *Serves 4*

1 tbsp olive oil
600g/1lb 5oz wild boar sausages, cut into quarters
1 onion, finely chopped
4 garlic cloves, finely chopped
2 carrots, roughly chopped
2 tbsp fresh thyme leaves
zest and juice of 1 blood orange
375ml/13fl oz white wine
100ml/3½fl oz vegetable stock (see p.23), if necessary
2 sprigs of fresh rosemary
2 tbsp dark rum
salt and freshly ground black pepper

METHOD

1. Heat the oil in a large frying pan and cook the sausages until they are brown on all sides. Lift the sausages out with a slotted spoon and set to one side, leaving the fat and oil in the pan.

2. Add the onion, garlic and carrots to the pan and cook for 1 minute, stirring, before adding the thyme. Cook until the onion has softened and started to brown. Tip the contents of the frying pan into the crock of the slow cooker.

3. Grate the zest of the orange over the vegetables, then lay the sausage quarters on top.

4. Pour the wine into the frying pan and stir to combine all the caramelized bits from the bottom. Bring to the boil and then pour over the contents of the slow cooker. If the sausages are not completely covered, add a little vegetable stock. Add the sprigs of fresh rosemary. Cover with the lid, turn the heat to HIGH and cook for 1 hour. Turn the heat to LOW and cook for a further 6 hours.

5. When the casserole is ready, remove the sausages and vegetables using a slotted spoon and put them on a warmed serving dish. Keep them warm while you prepare the gravy.

6. Discard the sprigs of rosemary and pour the juices from the slow cooker into a saucepan. Leave the liquid to settle and then remove as much fat from the surface as possible.

7. Pour the orange juice into the pan, add the rum and boil the liquid until it is reduced by half. Taste and season as necessary.

8. Spoon the sausages and vegetables on top of some mustard mash and pour the reduced gravy over the top.

CHEF'S TIP

To remove the last bit of fat from the surface of any liquid, either lay a double sheet of kitchen paper over the top or fold it several times lengthways and dip it just below the surface so that the paper absorbs all the excess fat.

WINTER WARMER

This spicy dish will warm all the extremities after a long walk on a cold winter's day. Just leave it to cook while you are out and you can come home to the wonderful aroma.

INGREDIENTS *Serves 6*

6 dried chipotle chillies
60g/2oz dried porcini mushrooms
200ml/7fl oz boiling water
100ml/3½fl oz chicken stock
3 tbsp olive oil
3 onions, finely chopped
2 garlic cloves, finely chopped
1 tsp dried oregano
1 tsp dried basil
1 tsp sweet paprika
6 boneless chicken breasts
400g/14oz can chopped tomatoes
salt and freshly ground black pepper

METHOD

1. Put the dried chillies and dried mushrooms in a bowl and cover with the boiling water. Leave for 30 minutes until they have become very soft. Drain, reserving the water.

2. Slit the chillies lengthways and scrape out the seeds. Chop the flesh roughly and put in a food processor. Add chicken stock to the reserved water to make it up to 300ml/10fl oz and add to the processor. Process until smooth.

3. Heat the oil in a frying pan, add the onions and cook over a medium heat until they are soft but not coloured. Add the garlic and cook for 1 minute.

4. Place the onions in the crock and add the oregano, basil and paprika. Brown the chicken in the frying pan, then place on top of the vegetables. Add the chilli sauce, soaked mushrooms and the tomatoes and season to taste. Cover with the lid and cook on HIGH for 3–4 hours, or until the chicken is tender and cooked right through.

PART 7

VEGETABLE DISHES

This section is not purely for vegetarians – the recipes are for everyone to try. Food doesn't need to contain meat to taste wonderful and with experimentation you'll find that by blending different flavours together, your vegetable dishes can take pride of place on the dinner table.

COOKING VEGETABLES

Vegetables all play a different role when used in cooking, whether it is done in a slow cooker or conventionally. Using a slow cooker, you benefit from tender vegetables without the risk of them being overcooked and mushy.

For the majority of these recipes, the onions are fried first in a little oil for about 5 minutes as these take the longest to cook out of any of the vegetables. Garlic, which is very pungent when raw, mellows considerably when cooked slowly, so don't be put off if a recipe uses a large quantity. Garlic is stronger when crushed or chopped, but if you would prefer a milder taste then just leave the clove whole or slice it rather than chopping.

Root vegetables do tend to take a long time to cook in a slow cooker, so make sure they are cut into small pieces and always place them at the bottom of the crock. Rinse vegetables such as potatoes in cold water before adding to the dish, as this will remove much of the starch. No matter which type of vegetables you are using, it's essential that they are totally immersed in liquid otherwise they will discolour and may remain hard.

Mushrooms can add a lot of flavour to a dish, particularly if you use dried ones, which will need to be soaked in boiling water before adding to the crock. If you are using a lot of mushrooms in a dish, reduce the amount of liquid slightly as mushrooms give off a lot of liquid during cooking.

Tomatoes work very well in slow cookers as they cook quickly and lose none of their colour or flavour. It is advisable to remove the skins and seeds of fresh tomatoes as these can go bitter.

AUBERGINE PARMIGIANA

This flavoursome Italian mixture of aubergines, tomatoes, peppers and cheeses can be served with your favourite pasta and a green salad.

INGREDIENTS *Serves 4*

2 large aubergines
2 tsp salt
2 eggs
75ml/2½fl oz water
3 tbsp plain flour
1 tbsp olive oil
60g/2oz fresh white breadcrumbs
60g/2oz Parmesan cheese, grated
350ml/11fl oz passata
115g/4oz jar sweet pimento, chopped
1 tsp dried mixed herbs
125g/4½oz mozzarella cheese, sliced
salt and freshly ground black pepper

METHOD

1. Cut the aubergines into 1cm/½in slices and place in layers in a bowl, sprinkling each layer with salt. Leave to stand for 30 minutes, then rinse and drain on kitchen paper.

2. Beat the egg with the water and flour to form a smooth batter.

3. Heat the olive oil in a large frying pan. Dip each slice of aubergine into the batter and then fry in the hot oil until lightly browned on each side. Drain on kitchen paper and set aside.

4. In a bowl, mix together the breadcrumbs and Parmesan cheese. In a separate bowl, combine the passata, chopped pimento and herbs.

5. In the crock, layer the aubergine slices, breadcrumb mixture, passata mixture and slices of mozzarella cheese. Season with salt and pepper and cook on LOW for 4 hours.

6. Serve as a side dish or stirred into your favourite pasta.

BIRYANI

Biryani was introduced to South Asia from Persia in the early 16th century and is a type of dry, spicy curry dish that can be made from almost any meat, fish or vegetable.

INGREDIENTS *Serves 4*

3 onions, finely chopped
2 garlic cloves, finely chopped
2.5cm/1in fresh root ginger, chopped
4 tbsp groundnut oil
1 small courgette, sliced
1 sweet red pepper, sliced
2 parsnips, chopped into 2cm/¾in pieces
1 tsp ground cumin
1 tsp garam masala
1 tsp ground coriander
1 tsp hot chilli powder
750ml/1¼ pint hot vegetable stock (see p.23)
salt and freshly ground black pepper
280g/10oz easy cook basmati rice
175g/6oz unsalted cashew nuts
45g/1½oz sultanas
2 tbsp chopped fresh coriander

METHOD

1. Put 1 onion, the garlic and the ginger into a food processor with 3 tablespoons of cold water and process until you have a smooth paste.

2. Heat 1 tablespoon of the oil in a frying pan and add the remaining onions. Fry gently for 10–15 minutes until they are soft and golden brown. Add the courgette, pepper and parsnips and cook for a further 3–4 minutes. Transfer the vegetables to the crock of your slow cooker.

3. Add 1 tablespoon of oil to the frying pan and cook the blended onion paste for 3–4 minutes, stirring so that it does not stick. Add the cumin, garam masala, coriander and chilli powder and cook for 1 minute. Gradually add a little of the hot stock to the

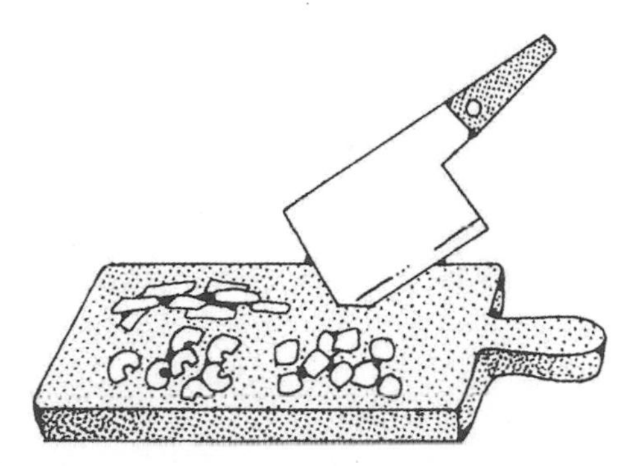

pan and stir to combine. Add this mixture to the crock and turn the slow cooker to HIGH. Add the remaining stock and season with salt and pepper, stirring to mix all the ingredients together. Cover with the lid and cook for 2–3 hours or until the vegetables are tender.

4. Towards the end of the cooking time, rinse and drain the rice and then parboil in lightly salted water for 3–4 minutes. Drain, and add to the slow cooker when the vegetables are cooked. Replace the lid and cook for a further hour until the rice is cooked and most of the liquid has been absorbed. If the mixture gets too dry, add a little more hot stock at this stage.

5. While the rice is cooking, put the remaining oil in a clean frying pan and fry the cashew nuts for about 2 minutes, stirring so they are lightly browned on all sides. Stir in the sultanas and fry for a further minute, or until they swell up. Remove the pan from the heat and transfer the nuts and sultanas to a piece of kitchen paper to drain off the oil.

6. Fold half the nuts and sultanas into the rice mixture in the slow cooker. Turn the cooker off, replace the lid and leave to stand for 5 minutes.

7. Spoon the biryani onto warmed serving dishes and scatter the remaining nuts and sultanas over the top. Garnish with chopped fresh coriander to finish.

BUTTERNUT SQUASH BAKE

Butternut squash are ripe at the end of autumn and their beautiful orange flesh adds a hint of sweetness to this dish.

INGREDIENTS *Serves 4*

350g/12oz wild rice
30g/1oz unsalted butter
1 onion, finely chopped
1 large butternut squash, peeled, deseeded and cut into cubes
450g/1lb button mushrooms, halved
1 carrot, sliced
1 turnip, diced
1 tsp dried marjoram
600ml/1 pint vegetable stock (see p.23)
1 tbsp fresh lemon juice
60g/2oz dried apricots, quartered
salt and freshly ground black pepper

METHOD

1. Rinse and drain the rice and then place in the crock of the slow cooker.

2. Melt the butter in a large frying pan and add the onion. Cook for 5 minutes or until the onion is soft but not brown. Add the squash, mushrooms, carrot and turnip and cook for another 4–5 minutes or until they start to soften.

3. Layer the vegetables on top of the rice and sprinkle on the dried marjoram.

4. Pour the stock and lemon juice over the top, cover with the lid and cook on LOW for 6–8 hours.

5. Half an hour before serving, add the dried fruit and season with salt and pepper.

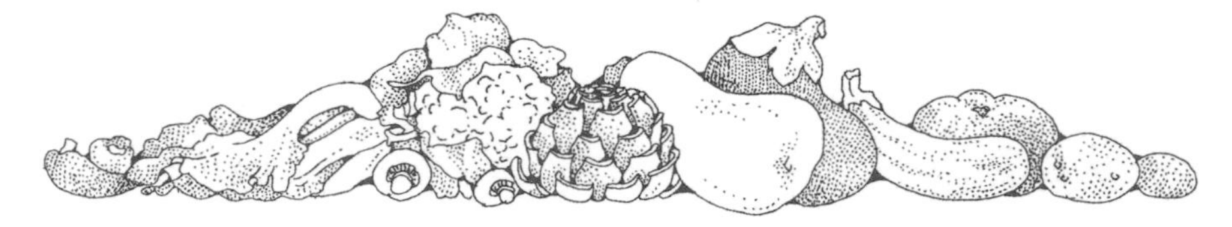

CAULIFLOWER & POTATO CURRY

Using a combination of spices to flavour vegetables makes a wonderful aromatic curry without the need for meat or fish.

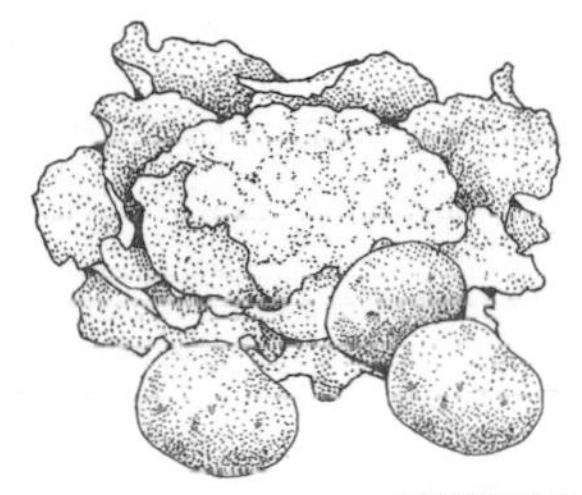

INGREDIENTS *Serves 4*

1 tbsp olive oil
1 large onion, finely chopped
3 garlic cloves, finely chopped
900g/2lb potatoes, peeled and cut into 2cm/¾in chunks
1 medium cauliflower, broken into small florets
¾ tsp ground turmeric
1½ tsp ground cumin
1 tsp ground coriander
1 tsp mustard seeds
1 tsp garam masala
½ tsp salt
1 tsp sugar
2 fresh tomatoes, skinned, seeded and roughly chopped
325ml/11fl oz vegetable stock (see p.23)

METHOD

1. Heat the olive oil in a large saucepan and add the onion. Cook for 5 minutes or until it is softened and starting to brown. Add the garlic and potato and cook for a further 5 minutes.

2. Blanch the cauliflower florets in boiling salted water for 2 minutes, then drain and transfer to the crock of your slow cooker. Add the onion and potato mixture along with all the spices, salt, sugar and tomatoes.

3. Bring the stock to boiling point in a saucepan and then pour it over the ingredients in the slow cooker. Cover with the lid and cook for 6 hours on LOW.

COUSCOUS-STUFFED PEPPERS

The bright colours of red and yellow sweet peppers stay vibrant even after several hours of cooking.

INGREDIENTS *Serves 4*
2 red sweet peppers
2 yellow sweet peppers

FOR THE STUFFING:
115g/4oz couscous
90ml/3fl oz boiling vegetable stock (see p.23)
1 tbsp olive oil
2 tsp fresh lemon juice
100g/3½oz plump raisins
3 tbsp toasted pine nuts
3 ripe tomatoes, skinned, deseeded and chopped
1 small red chilli, deseeded and finely chopped
2 tbsp chopped fresh parsley
85g/3oz feta cheese, crumbled
salt and freshly ground black pepper

METHOD

1. Slice the peppers lengthways and remove the seeds and membranes. Put them in a heatproof bowl and pour boiling water over them. Cover and leave to soften for 4 minutes.

2. Put the couscous in another bowl and pour the boiling vegetable stock over it. Leave to stand for 5 minutes or until all the fluid has been absorbed. Fluff it up with a fork then add the oil, lemon juice, raisins, pine nuts, tomatoes, chilli, parsley and feta cheese. Season to taste with salt and pepper.

3. Fill the peppers with the couscous mixture, making sure you press it down firmly. Put them in the crock of the slow cooker, filling-side up, then pour 150ml/5fl oz boiling water around them. Cover and cook on HIGH for 2–3 hours. Remove from the crock and brown under a hot grill before serving.

MACARONI CHEESE

With just a few ingredients you can make a wonderfully creamy macaroni cheese which can be put under the grill to brown.

INGREDIENTS *Serves 6*

225g/8oz uncooked macaroni
60g/2oz butter, cut into pieces
280g/10oz mature Cheddar cheese, grated
3 eggs, beaten
120ml/4fl oz sour cream
400ml/14fl oz can condensed Cheddar cheese soup
½ tsp salt
100ml/3½fl oz whole milk
½ tsp dry mustard
½ tsp black pepper
60g/2oz Cheddar cheese, grated
175g/6oz fresh wholemeal breadcrumbs

METHOD

1. Boil the macaroni in plenty of salted water until tender, following the manufacturer's recommended cooking time. Drain thoroughly.

2. In a separate saucepan, heat the butter and cheese, stirring until the cheese has melted. Pour this into the crock of your slow cooker and then add the beaten eggs, sour cream, cheese soup, salt, milk, mustard and pepper and stir well to combine.

3. Add the drained macaroni and stir again so that it is completely covered in the sauce. Cover with the lid, turn the setting to LOW and then cook for 3 hours, stirring once an hour to make sure that the macaroni stays covered in the sauce.

4. To make the topping, mix the grated cheese and breadcrumbs together and put on top of the cooked macaroni. Remove the crock from the slow cooker and put it under a preheated hot grill until the top of the macaroni cheese has turned golden brown and crispy.

NUT LOAF

If you fancy a change from a regular roast one Sunday, try this mixed nut loaf with a spicy tomato sauce.

INGREDIENTS *Serves 8*

60g/2oz unsalted butter
2 onions, finely chopped
225g/8oz button mushrooms, sliced
1 green pepper, deseeded and finely chopped
1 carrot, grated
1 celery stick, finely diced
5 eggs, beaten
85g/3oz walnuts, chopped
45g/1½oz sunflower seeds
½ tsp salt
½ tsp dried basil
½ tsp dried oregano
¼ tsp freshly ground black pepper
175g/6oz fresh wholemeal breadcrumbs

METHOD

1. Melt the butter in a large frying pan and add the onions. Cook for 5 minutes, or until they are soft and starting to go brown. Add the mushrooms, pepper, carrot and celery and cook for another 5 minutes.

2. Mix the remaining ingredients in a bowl and add the cooked vegetables.

3. Grease a rectangular loaf tin of a size that will fit your slow cooker and line with greaseproof paper. Press the ingredients into the tin, smoothing the surface with the back of a spoon. Cover the top with kitchen foil and secure with string.

4. Place a trivet or an upturned saucer in the crock, put the loaf tin on top and then pour in enough boiling water to come halfway up the sides of the tin. Cover and cook on HIGH for 4–5 hours or until the loaf has set. Leave the loaf to rest for 15 minutes before slicing.

POTATO LAYERS

This is a slow cooker variation on potato dauphinoise with scrumptious layers of potato, onion and cheese.

INGREDIENTS *Serves 4*

45g/1½oz butter
1 large onion, sliced into rings
4 garlic cloves, finely sliced
1 tsp dried thyme
900g/2lb waxy potatoes, very thinly sliced
salt and freshly ground black pepper
175g/6oz gruyère cheese, grated
400ml/14fl oz boiling vegetable stock (see p.23)
60ml/2fl oz double cream

METHOD

1. Grease the inside of the crock with a little of the butter.
2. Cover the bottom of the crock with a layer of onion, garlic and thyme, then cover with a layer of potatoes. Season and sprinkle some cheese over. Repeat these layers until you have used up all the ingredients except 2 tablespoons of cheese, ending with a layer of potato and cheese. Add a few knobs of butter to the top of the dish.
3. Pour in enough boiling vegetable stock to immerse the potatoes in liquid. Cover and cook on HIGH for 4–5 hours.
4. Thirty minutes before the potatoes will be ready, pour the cream over them. Replace the lid and cook for the last 30 minutes.
5. Just before serving, sprinkle some cheese over the top and place under a hot grill to brown.

CHEF'S TIP

To get really evenly sized slices of potato, use a vegetable mandolin.

PUMPKIN & WHITE BEAN LASAGNE

A quick and easy vegetable lasagne, this will surprise you with its unique blend of flavours and textures.

INGREDIENTS *Serves 4*

450g/1lb pumpkin flesh
30g/1oz butter, softened
400g/14oz ricotta cheese
6 quick-cook lasagne sheets
500ml/16fl oz tomato sauce (see p.24)
400g/14oz can haricot beans, drained
1 tbsp sun-dried tomatoes, finely chopped
115g/4oz mozzarella cheese, chopped

METHOD

1. Cut the pumpkin flesh into small cubes, drizzle with olive oil and roast in a preheated oven at 200°C/400°F/gas mark 6 for 20 minutes or until soft and lightly browned. Using a potato masher, mash the pumpkin until it has a smooth texture.

2. Grease the crock of your slow cooker with the butter. Mix the pumpkin with the ricotta cheese.

3. Soak the lasagne sheets in boiling water for 1 minute then drain. When cool enough to handle, cut off the corners so they fit the shape of your slow cooker.

4. Spread a thin layer of the tomato sauce over the base of the crock. Next, make a single layer of the lasagne sheets, followed by a layer of the pumpkin mixture. Spread another thin layer of sauce followed by a layer of beans sprinkled with the chopped sun-dried tomatoes. Repeat the above until you have used up all the ingredients, finishing with a layer of sauce.

5. Cook on LOW for 8 hours. Remove the crock from the slow cooker, distribute the mozzarella on top of the lasagne and melt under a hot grill before serving.

ROSEMARY POTATOES

This is a delicious way to cook potatoes using fresh rosemary. It makes a great accompaniment to any meat or fish dish.

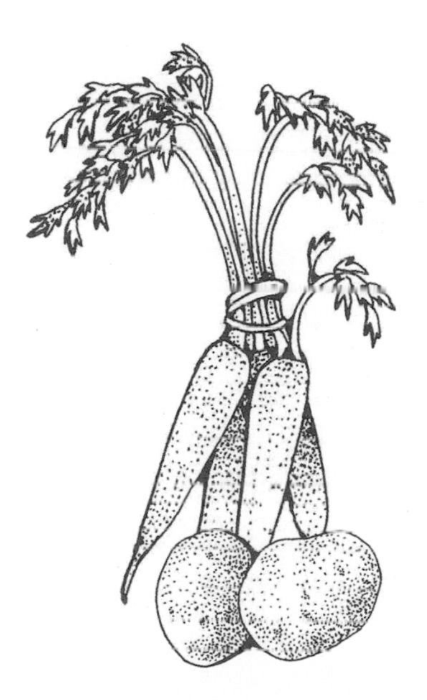

INGREDIENTS *Serves 6–8*

2 tbsp extra virgin olive oil
1 onion, coarsely chopped
8 potatoes, peeled and cut into wedges
8 baby carrots
1 tbsp finely chopped fresh rosemary leaves
½ tsp salt
½ tsp freshly ground black pepper

METHOD

1. Put 1 tablespoon of the olive oil in a large frying pan and add the onion. Fry for 4 minutes or until it is starting to soften.

2. Add the potato wedges and cook, constantly turning, so that they start to soften and become slightly brown on the outside. Add the baby carrots and cook for a further 3 minutes.

3. Brush the inside of the crock of your slow cooker with olive oil.

4. Put the potato mixture into the crock, sprinkle with the chopped rosemary and drizzle with the remaining oil.

5. Cover the slow cooker with the lid and cook on HIGH for 3–4 hours or until the potatoes are tender.

SPICED PARSNIPS

The addition of protein-rich chickpeas to this parsnip dish makes it a complete meal in itself.

INGREDIENTS *Serves 4*

4 garlic cloves, finely chopped
1 onion, finely chopped
5cm/2in fresh root ginger, finely chopped
2 red chillies, deseeded and finely chopped
75ml/2½fl oz cold water
4 tbsp sesame oil
1 tsp cumin seeds
2 tsp coriander seeds
1 tsp ground turmeric
½ tsp hot smoked paprika
60g/2oz cashew nuts, toasted and crushed
4 fresh tomatoes, skinned, deseeded and chopped
900g/2lb parsnips, cut into 2cm/¾in chunks
400g/14oz can chickpeas, drained
360ml/12fl oz boiling vegetable stock (see p.23)
salt and freshly ground black pepper
juice of 1 lime
chopped fresh coriander and whole toasted cashew nuts, to garnish

METHOD

1. Blend 3 garlic cloves, the onion, ginger, 1 chilli and the cold water in a food processor until you have a smooth paste.

2. Heat the oil in a large frying pan and add the cumin seeds. Cook for about 1 minute, then add the coriander, turmeric, paprika and crushed cashew nuts. Add the garlic and ginger paste and cook on high, stirring, until the spices give off their aromatic scent and the liquid has evaporated.

3. Add the tomatoes to the frying pan and cook for 1 more minute.

4. Tip the contents of the frying pan into the crock of your slow cooker. Add the parsnips and chickpeas and pour the boiling vegetable stock over. Stir to combine all the ingredients and season to taste with salt and pepper. Cover with the lid and cook on HIGH for 4 hours.

5. Remove the lid and stir in the lime juice and the remaining garlic and chilli. Replace the lid and cook for a further 30 minutes.

6. Spoon onto warmed serving plates and garnish with the chopped coriander and toasted cashew nuts. This is delicious served on warm flat breads (see right).

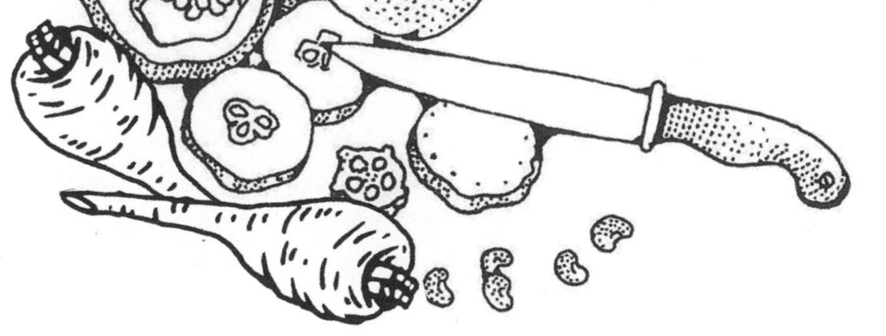

QUICK FLAT BREADS

450g/1lb wholemeal flour
250ml/8fl oz ice-cold water
3 tbsp olive oil
2 tsp salt
2 tsp baking powder
¼ tsp bicarbonate of soda

Combine all the ingredients and mix to a dough with your hands. Cut into 6 equal pieces and roll out to a thin 15cm/6in circle. Prick the surface with a fork and cook for a few minutes on an oiled hot griddle, turning once so that both sides are browned. Watch them carefully because this bread cooks rapidly.

SPICY RICE WITH SPINACH

This is a kind of risotto but using Indian spices and nuts and blended with baby spinach leaves.

INGREDIENTS *Serves 4*

280g/10oz brown rice
2 tbsp sunflower oil
30g/1oz unsalted butter
1 onion, finely chopped
2 garlic cloves, finely chopped
3 tomatoes, skinned, deseeded and roughly chopped
1 tsp ground coriander
1 tsp ground cumin
1 courgette, grated
1 carrot, grated
750ml/1¼ pint boiling vegetable stock (see p.23)
salt and freshly ground black pepper
175g/6oz baby spinach leaves
60g/2oz unsalted peanuts, toasted

METHOD

1. Rinse the rice under cold water, drain and tip into lightly salted boiling water. Cook for 4 minutes and drain well.

2. Heat the oil and butter in a frying pan and add the onion. Cook, stirring, for 5 minutes until soft. Add the garlic and tomatoes and cook for a further 2 minutes.

3. Add the rice to the pan together with the coriander and cumin and stir to combine.

4. Pour the rice mixture into the crock of your slow cooker. Stir in the grated courgette and carrot and pour in the boiling stock. Season with salt and pepper and stir to combine, then cover and cook on HIGH for 1 hour.

5. Lay the baby spinach leaves on top of the rice, replace the lid and cook for a further 40 minutes or until the rice is really tender.

6. Just before serving, stir the spinach into the rice. Spoon into warmed bowls and then sprinkle the toasted cashew nuts over the top.

SPICY VEGETABLE CURRY

Curries improve the longer you cook them, and using a slow cooker allows the flavours to infuse over a lengthy period.

INGREDIENTS *Serves 4*

2 carrots, sliced
1 sweet potato, peeled and cut into chunks
2 courgettes, sliced
1 sweet red pepper, deseeded and sliced
2 onions, finely chopped
3 garlic cloves, finely chopped
1 cauliflower, broken into florets
85g/3oz French beans, sliced
480ml/16fl oz vegetable stock (see p.23)
2 tbsp olive oil
1 tbsp tomato purée
1 tbsp curry powder
1 tsp sweet paprika
1 tsp ground ginger
1 tsp dried curry leaves
½ tsp sea salt
1 tsp ground cumin
1 tsp ground coriander
salt and freshly ground black pepper

METHOD

1. Prepare all the vegetables and layer them in the crock of the slow cooker.

2. Put the vegetable stock, olive oil, tomato purée and the spices in a saucepan and heat to a gentle simmer, stirring to mix all the flavours.

3. Pour the hot stock over the vegetables and season with salt and pepper.

4. Place the lid on the slow cooker, turn it onto the HIGH setting and leave the curry to cook for 4 hours.

5. Take off the lid and give the curry a gentle stir, then continue to cook on a LOW setting for a further 30 minutes. Serve with rice or flat naan breads.

SWEET POTATO BURRITOS

This economical and flavoursome recipe is served spooned into warmed tortillas and accompanied by sour cream.

INGREDIENTS *Serves 4*

1 tbsp hot chilli powder
2 tsp dried oregano
1½ tsp ground cumin
2 tbsp olive oil
1 onion, thinly sliced
1 large sweet potato, peeled and diced
4 garlic cloves, crushed
1 sweet red pepper, deseeded and finely chopped
1 red chilli, deseeded and finely chopped
400g/14oz can pinto beans, drained
200g/7oz can sweetcorn
3 tbsp fresh lime juice
1 tbsp chopped fresh coriander
85g/3oz Cheddar cheese, grated

METHOD

1. Combine the chilli powder, oregano and cumin in a small bowl and set aside.

2. Heat 1 tablespoon of the oil in a frying pan and cook the onion for 5 minutes, or until soft and lightly browned. Add the sweet potato, garlic, red pepper and chilli and cook for 3 more minutes, stirring. Add the pinto beans and sweetcorn and stir to combine.

3. Layer half the vegetables in the crock and sprinkle half the chilli mix over the surface. Make a second layer with the remaining vegetable and chilli mix. Drizzle the surface with the remaining olive oil, cover, and cook on LOW for 4–5 hours, or until the vegetables are tender.

4. Remove the lid and stir in the lime juice and fresh coriander.

5. Spoon into warm tortillas, add a layer of grated cheese and fold the tortilla in half. For those who can't handle the heat, serve with a good helping of sour cream.

SWEET POTATO CASSEROLE

Sweet potatoes make a wonderful alternative to potatoes. This recipe makes a lovely side dish with its crunchy pecan topping.

INGREDIENTS *Serves 6*

900g/2lb sweet potatoes, peeled and cut into chunks
150ml/5fl oz freshly squeezed orange juice
2 tbsp maple syrup
½ tsp ground cinnamon
½ tsp ground cardamom
½ tsp mustard seeds
salt and freshly ground black pepper

FOR THE TOPPING:
85g/3oz pecans, chopped
85g/3oz dark brown sugar
2 tbsp plain flour
60g/2oz butter

METHOD

1. Prepare the sweet potato, put it in a heatproof bowl and then pour enough boiling water over to just cover. Leave to stand for 5 minutes.

2. In another bowl, combine the orange juice, maple syrup, cinnamon, cardamom and mustard seeds and stir to mix.

3. Turn the slow cooker to HIGH and pour the orange juice mixture into the crock. Drain the sweet potatoes and add to the crock, stirring so that they are coated in the orange juice and spices. Season with salt and pepper and cook on HIGH for 4–5 hours or until the sweet potato is tender.

4. At the end of the cooking time, take a potato masher and gently crush the potato – you do not want them thoroughly mashed. Combine the topping ingredients and sprinkle over the top of the sweet potato. Remove the crock from the slow cooker, place under a hot grill and cook until the top is sizzling and brown.

VEGETABLE STEW WITH DUMPLINGS

This most definitely is a comfort food, with the perfectly soft, chewy cornmeal dumplings making it perfect for winter evenings.

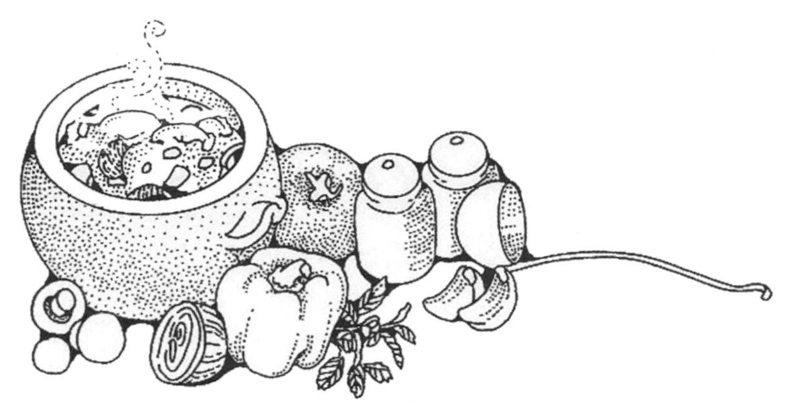

INGREDIENTS *Serves 6*

30g/1oz unsalted butter
1 large onion, sliced
4 garlic cloves, finely sliced
450g/1lb butternut squash, peeled, deseeded and cut into 1cm/½in cubes
2 large potatoes, peeled and cubed
1 fennel bulb, sliced
150g/5½oz button mushrooms, sliced
1 red pepper, deseeded and diced
2 × 400g/14oz cans chopped tomatoes
400g/14oz can butter beans, drained
1 tsp dried Italian seasoning
250 ml/8fl oz hot vegetable stock (see p.23)
salt and freshly ground black pepper
175g/6oz fresh garden peas

FOR THE DUMPLINGS:

85g/3oz plain flour
50g/1¾oz cornmeal

2 tbsp Parmesan cheese, grated
1 tbsp chopped fresh parsley
1 tsp baking powder
¼ tsp salt
1 egg
2 tbsp milk
2 tbsp vegetable oil
1 tsp hot smoked paprika

METHOD

1. Melt the butter in a frying pan and add the onion. Cook for 5 minutes until softened and just starting to brown. Add the garlic, squash, potatoes, fennel, mushrooms and pepper and cook for a further 2 minutes. Transfer to the crock of the slow cooker.

2. Add the tomatoes, butter beans and Italian seasoning and pour the hot vegetable stock over. Season to taste with salt and pepper. Stir to combine.

3. Cover with the lid and cook on HIGH for 4–5 hours or until the vegetables are all soft.

4. Towards the end of the cooking time, gather the ingredients together for the dumplings. Combine the flour, cornmeal, Parmesan cheese, parsley, baking powder and salt in a medium-sized bowl.

5. In a separate bowl, whisk together the egg, milk and vegetable oil.

6. Make a well in the middle of the flour mixture and pour the egg mixture into it. Mix with a fork to combine the ingredients and then knead with your hands until a smooth dough is formed. Break it into golf ball-sized pieces and roll into balls between the palms of your hands.

7. Turn your slow cooker to HIGH and add the garden peas. Stir well and then drop the dumplings onto the top of the stew. Sprinkle the tops of the dumplings with the paprika, replace the lid and cook for 1 hour. Do not lift the lid while the dumplings are cooking otherwise they will not rise and will be too heavy.

8. Spoon out onto warmed serving plates, dividing the dumplings evenly.

WINTER CHICKPEA CASSEROLE

If you want something to really warm you up on a chilly winter's evening, this casserole has it all.

INGREDIENTS *Serves 4*

1 tsp hot smoked paprika
1 tsp ground ginger
1 tsp hot curry powder
1 tsp turmeric
1 tsp garam masala
½ tsp ground black pepper
2 tbsp olive oil
1 large onion, chopped
115g/4oz feta cheese, crumbled
2 garlic cloves, crushed
2 fresh tomatoes, skinned, deseeded and chopped
250g/9oz dried chickpeas, rinsed and drained
1 tsp tamarind paste
1 tbsp Parmesan cheese, grated
½ butternut squash, peeled, deseeded and diced
10 green olives, pitted and halved
1 bay leaf
1 tbsp lemon juice
2 tbsp chopped fresh parsley
salt and ground black pepper

METHOD

1. Turn the slow cooker to HIGH. Add the spices, including the pepper, and cook for 15 minutes.

2. Stir in the olive oil and cook for 10 minutes. Add the onion and cook for an hour, or until soft and translucent.

3. Add the feta cheese, garlic, tomatoes, dried chickpeas, tamarind paste, Parmesan, squash, olives and bay leaf. Stir to combine, cover and cook for 4 hours on HIGH.

4. Remove the lid and stir in the lemon juice and parsley. Check for seasoning and add salt and pepper as necessary.

If you want to speed up this recipe by about an hour, fry the spices and onion in a little olive oil first, then add them to the slow cooker.

PART 8

CHUTNEYS & FRUIT CURDS

Although the slow cooker is unsuitable for making jams and jellies because the temperature is not high enough to obtain setting point, it can be used to make wonderful chutneys, pickles and fruit curds.

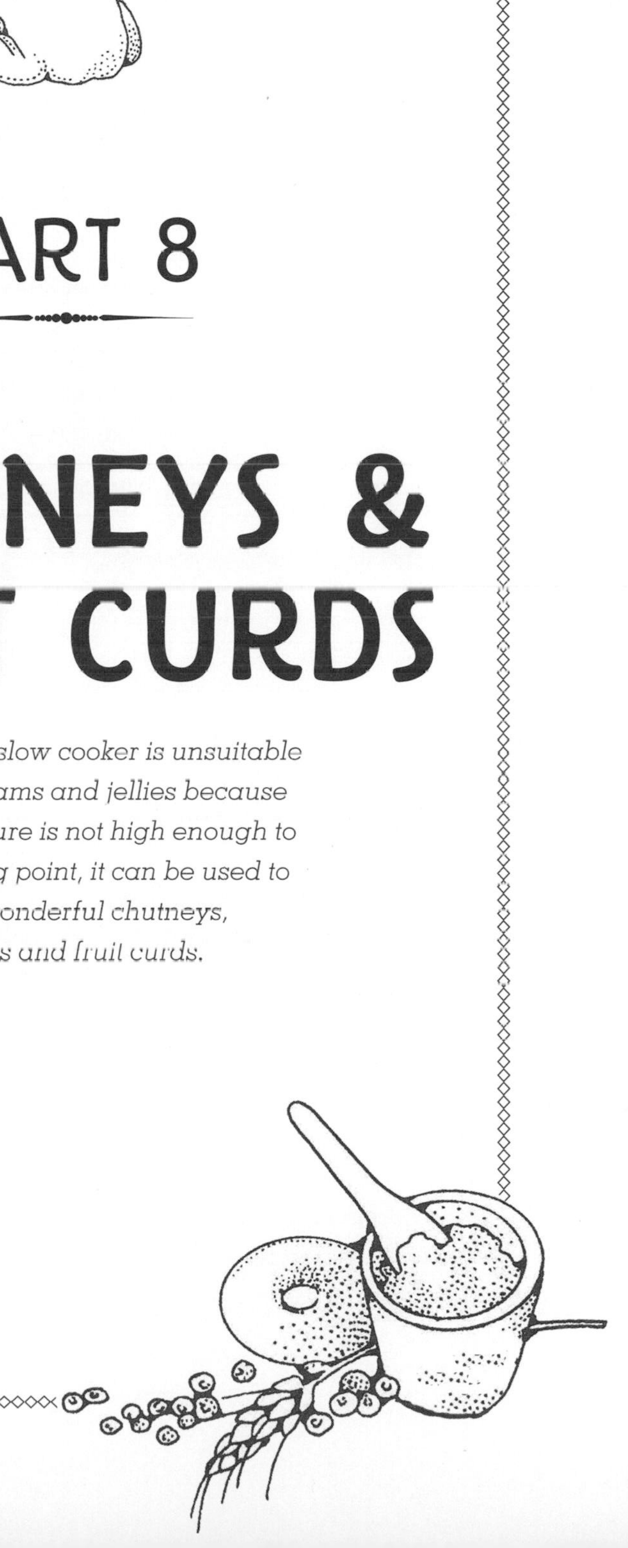

COOKING CHUTNEYS & FRUIT CURDS

The slow cooker is perfect for making moist chutneys because the long, slow cooking helps the flavours to develop so much that you don't have to wait weeks before eating.

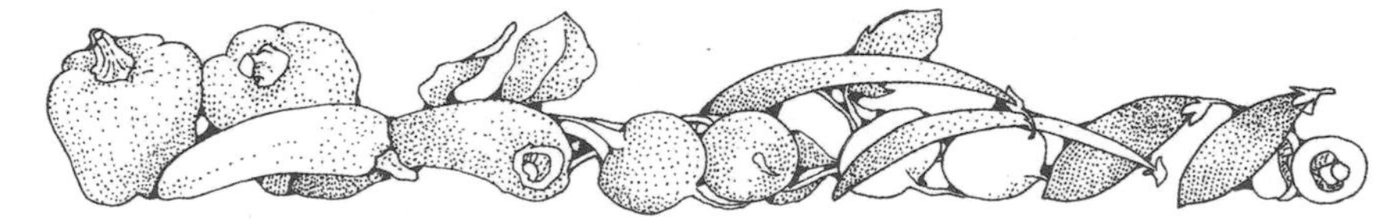

Fruit and vegetables retain their shape when cooked in a slow cooker, so you can make nice chunky chutneys to eat with cheese or cold meat without having to stay in for hours, stirring a preserving pan. The same thing applies to fruit curds, such as the well-known lemon curd. The slow cooker alleviates the need for constant stirring and the end result will be just as good as those made on top of the cooker.

Once you have made the chutneys or curds they will need to be stored in sterilized jars if you wish to keep them for any length of time. Never be tempted to put food into unsterilized jars as you risk contamination and the chutney going off very quickly. You can easily sterilize clean jars by placing them in a hot oven (180°C/350°F/gas mark 4) for 20 minutes, making sure they are not touching each other to allow heat to circulate all round.

Although the slow cooker is not suitable for the final stages of cooking jam and jellies, you can use it to soften the fruit at the beginning of the recipe, making sure you keep all of its natural flavour and nutrients.

APPLE CHUTNEY

Apple chutney is perfect for using up windfalls just as long as you remove any bruised or damaged portions first.

INGREDIENTS *Makes 1.35kg/3lb*

1.35kg/3lb cooking apples, peeled, cored and chopped
450g/1lb onions, roughly chopped
675g/1½lb demerara sugar
300ml/10fl oz malt vinegar
2 garlic cloves, crushed
1 tsp ground ginger
1 tsp cayenne pepper
1 tsp ground cinnamon
1 tsp hot curry powder
4 tsp sea salt

METHOD

1. Turn the slow cooker to HIGH and allow it to heat up while you are preparing the apples.

2. Place all the ingredients into the crock of your slow cooker and cook on HIGH for 30 minutes, uncovered, or until the sugar has dissolved. Stir, cover with the lid, and cook on HIGH for 9 hours, stirring occasionally, until the chutney has thickened. Continue to cook a little longer if there is too much liquid left.

3. At the end of the cooking time, give it a good stir and then transfer to warmed, sterilized jars and seal immediately.

VARIATION

Use 450g/1lb mixed fruit such as apricots, dates, figs and sultanas, putting them in the crock after the first 6 hours of cooking. Stir thoroughly and cook for the last 3 hours. You can also use 25g/1oz finely chopped fresh root ginger instead of ground ginger.

APRICOT & BUTTERNUT SQUASH

This chutney has a wonderful gold colour and quickly spices up a cheese platter or cheese on toast.

INGREDIENTS *Makes 1.8kg/4lb*

1 butternut squash (about 800g/1¾lb)
400g/14oz golden granulated sugar
300ml/10fl oz apple cider vinegar
225g/8oz dried apricots, chopped
grated zest and juice of 1 orange
2.5cm/1in fresh root ginger, peeled and grated
½ tsp ground turmeric
1 tbsp coriander seeds
2 tsp salt
115g/4oz toasted pine nuts

METHOD

1. Cut the butternut squash in half and remove the seeds with a spoon. Peel and cut into 1cm/½in cubes.

2. Put the sugar and vinegar into the crock of your slow cooker and turn the setting to HIGH. Leave to heat up for 30 minutes and then stir until the sugar has completely dissolved.

3. Stir in the remaining ingredients with the exception of the pine nuts, cover with the lid and cook for 5–6 hours, stirring from time to time. At the end of the cooking time the chutney should have thickened nicely, but if it is still a little runny, take the lid off and cook for a further hour so that the liquid can evaporate.

4. When the chutney is ready, stir in the toasted pine nuts and spoon into warm, sterilized jars. Seal immediately and leave to cool before labelling.

GREEN TOMATO & RHUBARB CHUTNEY

If you have a lot of green tomatoes left on the vine at the end of the summer use them up in this delicious chutney, which also includes some early autumn rhubarb.

INGREDIENTS *Makes 900g/2lb*

450g/1lb green tomatoes, sliced, or whole if cherry variety
450g/1lb rhubarb, cut into chunks
2 large red onions, sliced
225g/8oz cooking apples, peeled, cored and chopped (prepared weight)
115g/4oz raisins
2.5cm/1in fresh root ginger, finely chopped
120ml/4fl oz water
240ml/8fl oz red wine vinegar
675g/1½lb sugar
2 tsp ground allspice

METHOD

1. Put the tomatoes, rhubarb, onions, apples, raisins and ginger into the crock of your slow cooker with the water. Turn the setting to MEDIUM if your slow cooker has this setting, otherwise set it to HIGH. Allow the fruit and vegetables to soften for about 4 hours, but check after 3 hours if you are cooking on HIGH.

2. Increase the heat to HIGH (if applicable) and add the vinegar, sugar and allspice. Stir well, cover and cook for 6–8 hours, returning occasionally to give it a stir. The chutney is ready when it has turned a rich, brown colour and has thickened nicely. Adjust the cooking time as necessary.

3. When your chutney has thickened, transfer it to hot, sterilized jars and seal. Leave to cool before labelling.

LEMON CURD

Lemon curd is easy to make if you use your slow cooker as a *bain-marie* because the water doesn't become too hot and curdle the eggs.

INGREDIENTS *Makes 450g/1lb*

grated zest and juice of 3 lemons (unwaxed or organic)
200g/7oz granulated sugar
115g/4oz unsalted butter, diced
2 large eggs, plus 2 yolks

METHOD

1. Wash and dry the lemons. Finely grate the zest and then squeeze the juice out using a lemon squeezer, discarding any pips.

2. Pour approximately 5cm/2in of boiling water into the crock of your slow cooker and turn the setting to HIGH.

3. Put the lemon juice, grated zest, sugar and butter into a large heatproof bowl that fits comfortably inside the crock. Gently put the bowl inside the crock and add enough near-boiling water to come halfway up the sides of the bowl.

4. Leave the mixture in the cooker for about 15 minutes, uncovered, stirring occasionally until the sugar has dissolved and the butter has melted. Take the bowl out of the cooker and leave to cool for 5 minutes. Turn the cooker to LOW.

5. In a separate bowl, beat the eggs and extra egg yolks together and then strain them through a fine sieve into the lemon mixture. Whisk well until it is combined. Cover the bowl with kitchen foil and return it to the cooker. Cover and cook for 1 hour, stirring every 15 minutes. When it is thick enough to cover the back of a wooden spoon, it is ready. Spoon into hot, sterilized jars and seal.

MANGO & PEACH CHUTNEY

Mango chutney is often eaten to sweeten up fiery curries. This version is exceptionally easy to make and far nicer than any you can buy from a supermarket.

INGREDIENTS *Makes 900g/2lb*

900g/2lb peaches
3 firm mangoes
1 red onion, finely chopped
75ml/2½fl oz apple cider vinegar
200g/7oz soft brown sugar
1 jalapeño pepper, deseeded and finely chopped
2.5cm/1in fresh root ginger, peeled and finely chopped
2 garlic cloves, crushed
1 tsp Chinese 5-spice powder
½ tsp salt
85g/3oz raisins
2 bay leaves

METHOD

1. Cut the peaches in half, remove the stones and cut the flesh into small pieces.

2. Peel the mangoes, remove the large stones and chop the flesh into small pieces.

3. Put the fruit and onion into the crock of the slow cooker and add the cider vinegar. Stir, cover with the lid and cook on HIGH for 2 hours, stirring halfway through.

4. Stir in the sugar, jalapeño pepper, ginger, garlic, 5-spice powder, salt, raisins and bay leaves. Keep stirring until the sugar has completely dissolved. Cover and cook for a further 2 hours.

5. Remove the lid and cook for 1 hour or until the chutney has reduced to a thick consistency. Stir the chutney every 15 minutes during this last hour of cooking.

6. When you are happy with the consistency, remove the bay leaves and spoon the chutney into hot, sterilized jars. Seal immediately.

MINCEMEAT

Try this lovely cranberry mincemeat recipe at Christmas to make your mince pies and impress your guests.

INGREDIENTS *Makes 1.8kg/4lb*

500g/1lb 2 oz eating apples, peeled and cored
150ml/5fl oz brandy
115g/4oz dates, finely chopped
200g/7oz fresh cranberries
115g/4oz ready-to-eat apricots, chopped
60g/2oz almonds, chopped
1kg/2¼lb mixed dried fruit (raisins, sultanas, currants)
225g/8oz soft brown sugar
225g/8oz vegetable suet
3 tsp mixed spice
grated zest of 1 orange
grated zest of 1 lemon

METHOD

1. Dice the apples into cubes no larger than 3mm/⅛in.
2. Pour half the brandy into the crock of your slow cooker and add all the other ingredients. Set the slow cooker to HIGH. Stir the contents, cover with the lid and cook for 1 hour.
3. Remove the lid, stir, replace the lid and turn the setting to LOW. Cook for 2½ hours, stirring occasionally to prevent the mincemeat from sticking.
4. When the cooking time has finished, remove the lid, stir the mincemeat thoroughly and add the remaining brandy.
5. Spoon into hot, sterilized jars and cover with an airtight lid. Store in a cool place until required. Once the mincemeat has been opened it will need to be used up within 2 weeks.

SLOW-COOKED CARAMELIZED ONIONS

When onions are cooked slowly and allowed to absorb the flavours of balsamic vinegar they become sticky and sweet, making them a great accompaniment to anything savoury.

INGREDIENTS *Makes 450g/1lb*

2 tbsp olive oil
15g/½oz unsalted butter
500g/1lb 2oz onions, thinly sliced
salt and freshly ground black pepper
4 sprigs of fresh thyme
2 bay leaves
2 tbsp light brown sugar
2 tbsp balsamic vinegar
120ml/4fl oz red wine
60g/2oz dried apricots, chopped

METHOD

1. Turn the slow cooker to HIGH and allow it to heat up. Add the oil and butter to the crock and wait until the butter has melted.

2. Add the onions to the crock and stir to cover them in the butter mixture. Put the lid on the slow cooker and cook for 5 hours, stirring the mixture at least once an hour so that the onions brown evenly.

3. Season with salt and pepper and then add the thyme, bay leaves, sugar, balsamic vinegar, red wine and apricots. Stir with a wooden spoon until the sugar has dissolved then cover again and cook for 1½–2 hours or until the mixture is thick and sticky. You may need to stir it a few times during the last stage to stop it from sticking. Once ready, allow to cool and store in the refrigerator until ready to use.

SPICY FRUIT CHUTNEY

Because this recipe uses dried fruits it saves you all the hard work of peeling and chopping – the slow cooker will do the rest.

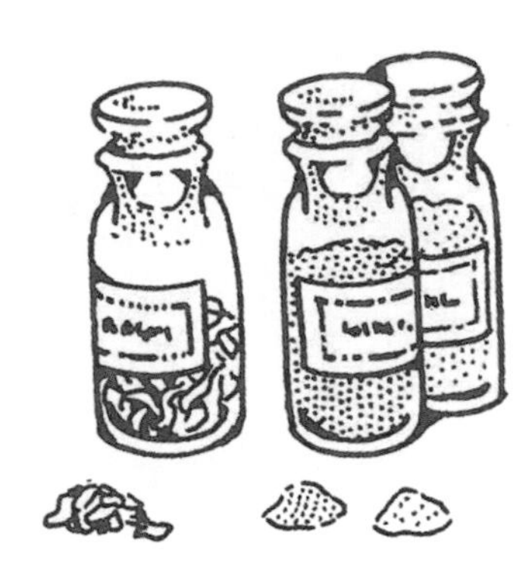

INGREDIENTS *Makes 675g/1½lb*

450g/1lb mixed dried fruit (peaches, apples, dates, mangoes and figs), coarsely chopped
450g/1lb dried apricots, coarsely chopped
85g/3oz raisins
1 onion, finely chopped
150g/5½oz brown sugar
500ml/16fl oz water
375ml/13fl oz cider vinegar
2 tsp Madras curry powder
½ tsp ground ginger
½ tsp cayenne pepper
¼ tsp salt

METHOD

1. Turn the slow cooker setting to HIGH and put the lid on.
2. Mix all the ingredients together and then place them in the slow cooker and cook, covered, on HIGH for 1–1½ hours.
3. Watch carefully towards the end of the cooking time because you want the fruit to be tender but also to hold its shape – if you overcook it, it will become mushy. Because you are not using raw fruit, this chutney cooks relatively quickly.
4. Spoon the chutney into hot, sterilized jars or allow it to cool and keep it in the refrigerator until you are ready to use it.

SWEET APPLE BUTTER

This homemade, slow-cooker version of apple butter is perfect on waffles, pancakes or hot buttered toast.

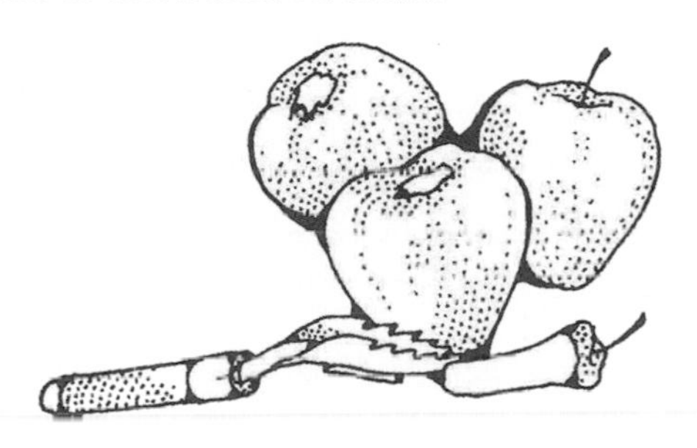

INGREDIENTS *Makes 900g/2lb*

100g/3½oz white sugar
100g/3½oz brown sugar
1½ tsp ground cinnamon
¼ tsp ground cloves
¼ tsp ground allspice
grated zest of 1 lemon
8 medium-sized eating apples, peeled, cored and finely chopped

METHOD

1. Turn the slow cooker to HIGH.

2. In a medium-sized bowl, blend the white and brown sugar, cinnamon, cloves, allspice and lemon zest.

3. Place the prepared apples in the crock of your slow cooker and then pour the sugar mixture over the top. Stir to combine all the ingredients. Put the lid on the slow cooker and cook on HIGH for about 11 hours. Check the apple mixture occasionally and give it a good stir. As it cooks the apple butter will start to go dark and thicken.

4. Once it has thickened, remove the lid and stir the apple butter again. Leave the lid off, reduce the heat to LOW and cook for a further 1–1½ hours.

5. Turn off the heat and allow the mixture to cool slightly before putting it into a blender. Process until you have a smooth purée. Put it into sterilized containers and, once cold, store in the freezer until you are ready to use it.

SWEET BROWN PICKLE

Very similar in taste to a traditional ploughman's pickle, this complements bread and cheese beautifully.

INGREDIENTS *Makes 1.8kg/4lb*

250g/9oz carrots, cut into 3mm/1/8in cubes
1 medium swede, peeled and cut into 3mm/1/8in cubes
4 garlic cloves, finely chopped
115g/4oz dates, finely chopped
1 small cauliflower, finely chopped
2 onions, finely chopped
2 eating apples, peeled, cored and finely chopped
1 courgette, cut into 3mm/1/8in cubes
225g/8oz dark brown sugar
1 tsp salt
½ tsp ground black pepper
4 tbsp lemon juice
250ml/8fl oz malt vinegar
1 tbsp Worcestershire sauce
2 tsp mustard seeds, toasted and ground
2 tsp ground allspice
½ tsp cayenne pepper

METHOD

1. Turn the slow cooker to HIGH.
2. Combine all the ingredients in the crock of your slow cooker and cook for 30 minutes, uncovered, stirring until the sugar has dissolved completely.
3. Cover with the lid and cook for 3 hours until all the vegetables are tender.
4. Remove the lid and continue to cook on HIGH, stirring occasionally, until the liquid has evaporated and the pickle has thickened.
5. Spoon into hot, sterilized jars and seal. The flavour of this pickle will improve with keeping, but if you can't wait a couple of weeks it will still taste good.

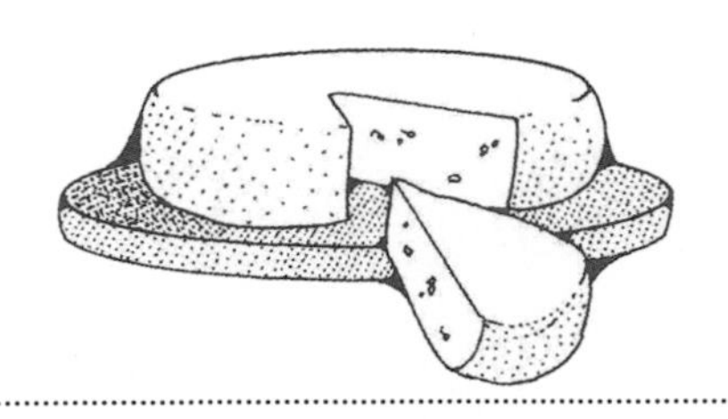

PART 9

PUDDINGS & CAKES

The slow cooker is perfect for making steamed puddings, custards and even cakes. The moist atmosphere makes puddings such as a steamed syrup sponge incredibly light and all you need are a few bowls and tins that will fit inside your crock.

MAKING PUDDINGS & CAKES

However satiated we may feel after a main course, somehow we always find room for a sweet pudding to finish off the meal. The slow cooker can create these for you without your having to stand and watch that the water doesn't bubble up and spoil the pudding.

Crock pots are ideal for anyone who loves baking but doesn't have time to monitor the cooking process. It is worth investing in a special baking rack to go in the base of the crock to stand your dishes on, as the majority of the recipes in this section are cooked by the *bain-marie* method. This is very important as the heat needs to circulate all around the bowl or tin. If you are only just starting out you can get by with an upturned saucer or by crumpling up some kitchen foil so that the dish is raised about 2.5cm/1in from the bottom of the crock.

When you are making sponge puddings and cakes it is important that all your ingredients are at room temperature before you start, otherwise you may find that the cake or pudding won't rise and will have a heavy consistency.

You will need to avoid lifting the lid during the cooking time because this will release some of the heat built up inside. Take care when removing the dish from the crock as it will be exceptionally hot, so make sure you have oven gloves handy.

BAKED APPLES

Using crumbled gingernut biscuits as a stuffing gives these baked apples a delicate flavour to complement the fruit and nuts.

INGREDIENTS *Serves 4*

85g/3oz butter, softened
3 tbsp cloudy apple juice
85g/3oz soft brown sugar
¼ tsp ground cinnamon
grated zest and juice of ½ orange
2 tbsp crushed gingernut biscuits
30g/1oz unsalted cashew nuts, finely chopped
30g/1oz raisins
30g/1oz dried cranberries
4 large cooking apples such as Bramleys

METHOD

1. Grease the inside of the crock with some of the butter, pour in the apple juice and turn the setting to HIGH.
2. Put the remaining butter in a bowl and add the sugar, cinnamon, orange zest and juice and crushed gingernuts and stir well to combine.
3. Add the cashews, raisins and cranberries, mix well and set aside.
4. Remove the cores of the apples using an apple corer and then push it in a few more times to make the cavity about twice the original size. Take a sharp knife and score the skin all the way round the middle of the apples.
5. Divide the fruit filling equally between the apples and stuff it into the central cavities, allowing the stuffing to overflow at the top.
6. Stand the apples in the crock, cover with the lid and turn the heat down to LOW. Cook for 4 hours or until the apples are cooked all the way through. You may need to increase the cooking time if your cooking apples are very large.

BANANAS WITH RUM & RAISINS

An exceptionally easy dessert to prepare, this is totally irresistible as the sauce starts to turn sticky as it cooks.

INGREDIENTS *Serves 4*

2 tbsp seedless raisins
3 tbsp dark rum
45g/1½oz unsalted butter, diced
60g/2oz soft brown sugar
4 bananas, not too ripe
¼ tsp ground cinnamon
¼ tsp ground ginger
30g/1oz pecans, finely chopped

METHOD

1. Put the raisins in a bowl and cover them with 2 tablespoons of the rum. Set them to one side to soak.

2. Place the butter in the crock of your slow cooker. Add the remaining rum and the sugar and set the cooker to HIGH. Leave to heat up, uncovered, for about 15 minutes or until the butter has melted. Stir until the sugar has dissolved.

3. Peel the bananas and cut them in half lengthways. Lay them on top of the syrup in the crock, cover with the lid and cook for 30 minutes or until the fruit is almost tender. After 15 minutes, carefully turn the bananas over.

4. Sprinkle the cinnamon and ginger over the bananas and then add the raisins and the rum they were soaked in. Mix gently to combine the ingredients, cover, and cook for another 10 minutes.

5. Lift the bananas very carefully out of the slow cooker, place them on warmed individual serving plates and drizzle with the syrup. Sprinkle with the finely chopped pecans and serve while still hot with some whipped cream or ice cream.

BREAD & BUTTER PUDDING

This version of bread and butter pudding uses Italian panettone to give the final dish a taste of luxury.

INGREDIENTS *Serves 4*
45g/1½oz butter
6 slices panettone, 1 day old and crusts removed
85g/3oz raisins
60g/2oz dates, chopped
3 eggs, beaten
60g/2oz caster sugar
300ml/10fl oz whole milk
seeds of 1 vanilla pod
freshly grated nutmeg
2 tbsp demerara sugar

METHOD
1. Grease a 1 litre/1¾ pint oval dish with butter, checking that it will fit inside your slow cooker.
2. Pour almost-boiling water into the crock of your slow cooker to a depth of about 2.5cm/1in and place an upturned saucer or cooking rack on the base.
3. Butter one side of the panettone slices and then cut them in half diagonally. Overlap the bread slices in the oval dish, buttered-side up. Scatter the raisins and dates over the bread.
4. In a separate bowl, whisk together the eggs and sugar. Gradually whisk in the milk, vanilla, and some nutmeg.
5. Place the oval dish inside your slow cooker and then pour the egg mixture over the bread. Push the bread down so that it is thoroughly soaked in the egg mixture. Sprinkle the surface with the demerara sugar and a little extra grated nutmeg.
6. Pour boiling water around the dish to a depth of halfway up the sides. Put the lid on and cook on HIGH for 3–4 hours or until the custard is set. If you like the top crunchy, remove the dish from the slow cooker and place under a hot grill to brown.

CARROT & COURGETTE CAKE

The combination of carrot and courgette makes this cake very light and crumbly and totally irresistible.

INGREDIENTS *Serves 8*

butter for greasing
175g/6oz butter, softened
175g/6oz light brown sugar
3 eggs, lightly beaten
85g/3oz carrot, grated
85g/3oz courgette, grated
grated zest of 1 orange
60g/2oz sultanas
115g/4oz self-raising flour
1 tsp baking powder
½ tsp ground cinnamon
½ tsp freshly grated nutmeg

FOR THE CREAM CHEESE ICING:
300g/10oz icing sugar
50g/1¾oz unsalted butter, at room temperature
125g/4½oz cream cheese, cold

METHOD

1. Place an upturned saucer or cooking rack in the base of your slow cooker, pour in 2.5cm/1in of very hot water and turn the setting to HIGH.

2. Generously grease a deep, round, fixed-based cake tin (18cm/7in diameter) with butter and line the base with greaseproof paper.

3. In a bowl, cream together the butter and sugar until light and creamy. Gradually add the lightly beaten eggs, beating after each addition. Stir in the grated carrot and courgette, orange zest and sultanas.

4. Sift the flour, baking powder and spices together and then add to the bowl. Gradually fold to combine the flour, but do not overwork at this stage.

5. Spoon the cake mixture into the tin and level off the surface with the back of a spoon. Cover the tin with a layer of greased kitchen foil and then place

carefully inside the slow cooker on top of the upturned saucer or rack. Pour boiling water around the tin to a depth of halfway up the sides.

6. Put the lid on the slow cooker and cook for 3–5 hours, or until a skewer inserted into the middle of the cake comes out clean. Lift the cake tin out of the slow cooker using a pair of oven gloves and leave to cool for 5 minutes. Turn the cake out onto a wire rack to cool.

7. To make the icing, sift the icing sugar into a bowl and then add the softened butter. Using a hand mixer, beat the mixture on medium speed until it comes together and is creamy in texture.

8. Add the cream cheese and beat until it is completely mixed into the icing mixture. Continue to beat at high speed until the icing is light and fluffy. As soon as it reaches this stage, stop beating otherwise the icing can become runny.

9. Once the icing has completely cooled, spread it on the top and sides of the cake.

10. Decorate the top of the cake with halved walnuts or pecans or, if it is for a special occasion, sink some fresh strawberries into the icing and dust with icing sugar.

CHOCOLATE & BANANA PUDDING

This steamed pudding is served with a rich caramel sauce – sheer indulgence at the end of a meal.

INGREDIENTS *Serves 4*

85g/3oz unsalted butter, diced, plus extra for greasing
200g/7oz self-raising flour
2 ripe bananas
85g/3oz golden caster sugar
1 egg, lightly beaten
60ml/2fl oz semi-skimmed milk
85g/3oz dark chocolate chips

FOR THE CARAMEL SAUCE:

115g/4oz unsalted butter
115g/4oz soft brown sugar
3 tbsp milk
60ml/2fl oz double cream

METHOD

1. Butter a 1 litre/1¾ pint pudding basin and line the base with baking parchment. Place an upturned saucer or cooking rack in the crock of your slow cooker and add 2.5cm/1in of boiling water. Turn the setting to HIGH.

2. Sift the flour into a large bowl and rub in the diced butter using your fingertips until the mixture resembles fine breadcrumbs.

3. In another bowl, mash the bananas and then stir them into the flour mixture. Add the sugar and mix well.

4. Beat the egg with the milk and gradually add to the bowl with the flour and banana mixture, beating well between each addition. Gently fold in the chocolate chips and then spoon the mixture into the prepared pudding basin. Cover with a layer of greased kitchen foil and then place the basin carefully into the crock so that it stands on the upturned saucer or cooking rack.

5. Pour boiling water around the pudding basin to a depth of halfway up the sides. Cover

with the lid and cook on HIGH for 3–4 hours. When the pudding is cooked, a skewer inserted into the centre will come out clean.

6. Turn off the slow cooker and leave the pudding in the warm water while you make the caramel sauce.

7. To make the sauce, put the butter, sugar and milk into a small saucepan and bring it slowly to the boil. Simmer for 2 minutes and then remove it from the heat. Allow it to cool slightly and then add the cream and stir until you have a thick, creamy sauce.

8. Carefully turn the pudding out onto a serving plate and then pour the caramel sauce over the top.

VARIATION

Try chocolate sauce in place of the caramel:

115g/4oz milk chocolate, broken into squares
115g/4oz dark chocolate, broken into squares
250ml/8fl oz double cream

Melt the chocolate in a bowl set over hot water and gradually add the cream.

FRAGRANT STEWED RHUBARB

This is a pudding that can be left to stew in its own juices while you are out at work. It is wonderful spooned over ice cream or yogurt, or used as a base for crumble.

INGREDIENTS *Serves 4–6*
600g/1lb 5oz rhubarb
120ml/4fl oz water
175ml/6fl oz runny honey
5cm/2in fresh root ginger, grated

METHOD

1. Wash the rhubarb under cold water and cut off the stems. Pull off any stringy bits and cut into 2.5cm/1in slices.

2. Put all the ingredients in the slow cooker, stir and cover with the lid. Cook on LOW for 6–8 hours or until the rhubarb is falling apart.

VARIATION

Here is another recipe for stewed rhubarb but this time it is complemented by the addition of fresh strawberries.

250g/9oz rhubarb, sliced
250g/9oz fresh strawberries, sliced
175g/6oz caster sugar
2 tsp lemon juice

Wash and prepare the fruit and then place all the ingredients in the slow cooker. Cover and cook on LOW for 6–8 hours until the fruit is tender.

HEAVENLY BAKED CUSTARD

This baked custard is so creamy it will melt in your mouth and the sweetness of the maple syrup makes it extra special.

INGREDIENTS *Serves 6*

3 eggs
120ml/4fl oz maple syrup
250ml/8fl oz whole milk
150ml/5fl oz single cream
1 vanilla pod
½ tsp freshly grated nutmeg

METHOD

1. Beat the eggs in a large bowl and then whisk in the maple syrup.

2. Warm the milk and cream until hand hot and then gradually whisk into the egg mixture.

3. Split the vanilla pod, scrape out the seeds using the blade of a knife and add to the custard mixture along with the grated nutmeg.

4. Pour the custard into 6 individual ramekin dishes, first making sure they will fit into the crock of your slow cooker in a single layer. Cover each ramekin with a piece of kitchen foil and secure tightly.

5. Put the ramekins into the crock and pour in boiling water to a depth of three-quarters of the way up the sides of the ramekins. Cover with the lid and cook on LOW for 2½–3 hours or until the custard has set. To test if it is ready, insert a skewer into the centre of one of the ramekins; it will come out clean when the custard is set.

6. When ready, remove the ramekins carefully as they will be hot and place them to cool on a wire rack. Put them in the refrigerator to chill and take them out 30 minutes before you are ready to serve.

7. Top each ramekin with a few fresh raspberries or sliced strawberries.

MOIST GINGER CAKE

Because this cake is steamed in the slow cooker it retains its moisture and all the flavours are allowed to mature without your having to wait a few days. Using golden syrup instead of treacle gives a lovely sticky texture.

INGREDIENTS *Serves 6–8*

100g/3½oz butter, plus extra for greasing
100g/3½oz dark brown sugar
100g/3½oz golden syrup
100g/3½oz dates, stoned and chopped
100g/3½oz plain flour
100g/3½oz self-raising flour
½ tsp bicarbonate of soda
2 tsp ground ginger
3 pieces stem ginger, finely chopped
2 eggs, at room temperature, beaten
100ml/3½fl oz semi-skimmed milk, at room temperature
chopped stem ginger, to decorate

FOR THE ICING:
125g/4½oz icing sugar
3 tsp lemon juice

METHOD

1. Butter a 15cm/6in circular cake tin with a fixed base and line the base with a circle of non-stick baking parchment. Pour 2.5cm/2in of very hot water into the base of the crock and turn the setting to HIGH.

2. Put the butter, sugar, syrup and dates into a saucepan and heat gently, stirring, until the butter and sugar have melted. Take the pan off the heat and add the flours, bicarbonate of soda, ground ginger, finely chopped stem ginger, eggs and milk and beat until the mixture is smooth.

3. Pour the cake mixture into the prepared tin and cover with buttered kitchen foil. Carefully place the tin inside the crock and slowly pour in very hot water until it comes halfway up the sides of the tin.

4. Cover with the lid and cook on HIGH for 4½–5 hours. The cake will be cooked when a skewer inserted in the middle comes out clean.

5. Carefully lift out the tin from the slow cooker and leave to rest for 10 minutes. Loosen the edges of the cake with a knife, then turn it out onto a wire rack. Peel off the baking parchment and leave to cool.

6. To make the icing, sift the icing sugar into a bowl and add just enough lemon juice to make a smooth, thick icing. Spoon over the cake and spread evenly. Decorate the surface with small pieces of stem ginger.

VARIATIONS

- For a darker version of this cake, use treacle in place of the golden syrup and add 30g/1oz of malt extract to retain the stickiness.
- If you are not keen on dates you can replace them with sultanas, raisins or some cooking apple chopped into small pieces.
- Experiment with some different-flavoured icings.

POACHED PEARS

Pears poached in red wine take on a lovely rosy hue and absorb all the flavours of the spice and maple syrup.

INGREDIENTS *Serves 6*

75cl bottle fruity red wine
100g/3½oz soft brown sugar
120ml/4fl oz maple syrup
1 cinnamon stick
1 vanilla pod, split lengthways
2 strips of orange zest
2 whole cloves
½ tsp ground ginger
6 firm ripe pears
2 tbsp lemon juice

METHOD

1. Pour the red wine into the crock of your slow cooker and turn the heat to HIGH. Add the sugar, maple syrup, cinnamon stick, vanilla pod, orange zest, cloves and ginger. Cook for 30 minutes, stirring occasionally.

2. Peel the pears using a vegetable peeler so that you do not remove too much of the flesh. Using an apple corer, remove their cores, starting at the base and leaving the stalk intact. As soon as each pear is ready, roll it round in the lemon juice to stop it from discolouring.

3. Place the pears in the wine mixture in the slow cooker, stalk side up. Cover with the lid and cook for 2–4 hours, turning the pears occasionally to make sure they are always covered in the liquid. The pears should be just tender but not too soft.

4. Remove the pears using a slotted spoon and put them on a serving plate. Continue to cook the wine mixture, uncovered, for a further hour or until it has reduced and started to thicken. (If you wish to save time you can reduce the liquid in a saucepan over a high heat.) Strain the liquid over the pears and chill in the fridge until ready to serve.

RICE PUDDING

Because a rice pudding needs to be cooked at a low temperature it is sometimes inconvenient when other dishes require the oven to be hotter. You can easily get round this problem by cooking the rice in your slow cooker. The only difference is that it will not form a skin on the surface.

INGREDIENTS *Serves 4*
butter, for greasing
115g/4oz pudding rice
60g/2oz caster sugar
30g/1oz butter
1.2 litre/2 pints whole milk
½ tsp freshly grated nutmeg

METHOD

1. Butter the inside of your crock and then add all the ingredients, stirring so that they are all mixed thoroughly.

2. Turn the cooker to HIGH, cover with the lid and cook for 3–4 hours. Remove the lid and give the pudding a good stir.

3. Replace the lid and reduce the setting to LOW. Cook for a further 5–6 hours or until the rice is cooked and most of the liquid has been absorbed. Give the pudding a stir a couple of times during the last few hours of cooking to make sure it is not sticking to the bottom.

VARIATIONS

- Add 60g/2oz raisins to give a fruity taste.
- To make the pudding sweet and creamy, substitute 175ml/6fl oz evaporated milk for fresh milk.
- For a really creamy version, use half milk and half single cream.

SLOW-COOKER CHEESECAKE

A cheesecake made in the slow cooker has an amazingly silky texture and can be topped with any fresh fruit you like.

INGREDIENTS *Serves 6*

FOR THE CRUST:

85g/3oz digestive biscuits
3 tbsp butter, melted
2 tbsp soft brown sugar
1 tsp ground cinnamon

FOR THE FILLING:

450g/1lb cream cheese, softened to room temperature
150g/5½oz sugar
3 eggs
1 tbsp plain flour
250ml/8fl oz sour cream
1 tsp grated lemon zest
1 tsp almond essence

METHOD

1. Place an upturned saucer or cooking rack in the crock, pour in 2.5cm/2in boiling water and turn the heat to HIGH. Grease a 600ml/1 pint soufflé dish.
2. Put the digestive biscuits inside a large freezer bag, seal it and then crush them using a rolling pin. Tip the crumbs into a bowl and add the melted butter, sugar and cinnamon. Mix until the crumbs start to hold together.
3. Firmly press the crumb mixture into the base of the soufflé dish.
4. In a separate bowl, cream together the cheese, sugar, eggs, flour, sour cream, lemon zest and almond essence until creamy and smooth. Spoon the filling on top of the biscuit crumb.
5. Carefully lower the dish into the crock and add boiling water to a depth of halfway up the sides of the dish.
6. Line the lid of the slow cooker with a few layers of kitchen paper to absorb excess moisture and cook on HIGH for 3 hours. The cheesecake is cooked when the mixture has set.

STICKY TOFFEE PUDDING

This recipe for toffee pudding is so delectable the family will keep coming back for more.

INGREDIENTS *Serves 6*

175g/6oz dates, stoned and finely chopped
175ml/6fl oz hot water
½ tsp bicarbonate of soda
140g/5oz self-raising flour
½ tsp salt
150g/5½oz soft brown sugar
2 eggs, beaten
1 tsp vanilla essence
4 tbsp unsalted butter, melted

METHOD

1. Place an upturned saucer or cooking rack in the crock, pour in 2.5cm/2in boiling water and set to HIGH. Grease and flour a 600ml/1 pint pudding basin.
2. Put the dates in a bowl, add the hot water and bicarbonate of soda and leave to soak for 5 minutes to soften the skins.
3. Sift the flour and salt into a bowl. Drain the dates and put into a food processor with the sugar, eggs and vanilla essence and process until smooth. With the food processor running, add the butter and process until smooth. Gradually fold in the flour and then pour the batter into the prepared basin.
4. Place in the crock and add boiling water to reach halfway up the sides of the bowl. Cook on HIGH for 2½–3 hours. The pudding is ready when it springs back when pressed with a finger.

TOFFEE SAUCE

For the toffee sauce, melt 115g/4oz butter with 200g/7oz brown sugar and 175ml/6fl oz double cream over a gentle heat. Once it starts to bubble, give it a good whisk and pour over the pudding. For adults, add 1 tablespoon dark rum to the sauce.

SYRUP SPONGE PUDDING

Syrup sponge pudding is a favourite with all ages and one that will never lose its pride of place on the dessert menu.

INGREDIENTS *Serves 4*
butter, for greasing
4 tbsp golden syrup
115g/4oz self-raising flour
¼ tsp salt
60g/2oz caster sugar
60g/2oz vegetarian suet
1 egg, beaten
2 tbsp semi-skimmed milk

METHOD

1. Place an upturned saucer or cooking rack in the base of your slow cooker and pour in 2.5cm/1in boiling water. Turn the setting to HIGH.

2. Butter a 600ml/1 pint pudding basin and spoon the golden syrup into the base. If you warm your spoon first under hot water you will find the syrup runs off easily.

3. Sift the flour and salt into a bowl and add the sugar and suet. Using your fingertips, combine the ingredients. Gradually mix in the egg and milk until the mixture is smooth.

4. Spoon the mixture into the pudding basin and cover it with a layer of greased kitchen foil, putting a fold in the centre to give the pudding room to rise.

5. Carefully place the pudding basin on top of the saucer in the slow cooker and pour in boiling water to come about halfway up the sides of the basin. Cover with the lid and cook on HIGH for 3–4 hours or until the pudding springs back when you touch the surface.

6. Turn off the heat, remove the bowl from the slow cooker and leave to cool for 5 minutes. Remove the foil and, using a sharp knife, loosen the edges of the pudding and turn it out onto a plate – be careful as the syrup will be exceptionally hot!

TOFFEE APPLES

This is a really good recipe for a children's party and you can even ask older children to help you dip the apples.

INGREDIENTS *Makes 8*

2 × 400g/14oz packets of caramels
60ml/2fl oz water
8 eating apples
butter, for greasing

METHOD

1. Put the caramels and water in the crock of your slow cooker. Cover with a lid and cook on HIGH for 1–1½ hours or until the caramels have melted. Stir every 15 minutes to stop them sticking.
2. Turn the slow cooker setting to LOW.
3. Wash the apples and dry on kitchen paper. Line a baking tray with greaseproof paper and grease it with butter to stop the apples from sticking to it.
4. Push a wooden stick into the base of each apple so that it goes almost all the way to the top.
5. Dip an apple into the hot caramel, turning it so that the whole surface is covered. Holding the apple above the crock, scrape off any excess caramel.
6. Put the apple on the baking tray and repeat with the remaining apples. When all are ready, put them in the fridge for the caramel to set thoroughly.

CAUTION

If you are asking your children to help you dip the apples you need to remember that the crock and the caramel will be scalding hot. Protect children's hands with a pair of gloves.

INDEX